Pensford, Publow and Woollard

A Topographical

Rowland Janes

biografix.co.uk

First Published in Great Britain as
'Publow Field Names' (1989)
© Rowland Janes
Published by The Becket Centre, Pensford

This revised edition published as
'Pensford, Publow and Woollard - A Topographical History' (2003)
© Rowland Janes
Published by Biografix
Stowey, Somerset, BS39 5TH
www.biografix.co.uk
info@biografix.co.uk

ISBN 0-9545125-0-2

Design and typesetting by Biografix, Somerset
Printed and bound by the Cromwell Press, Wiltshire

All rights reserved

PUBLOW PARISH

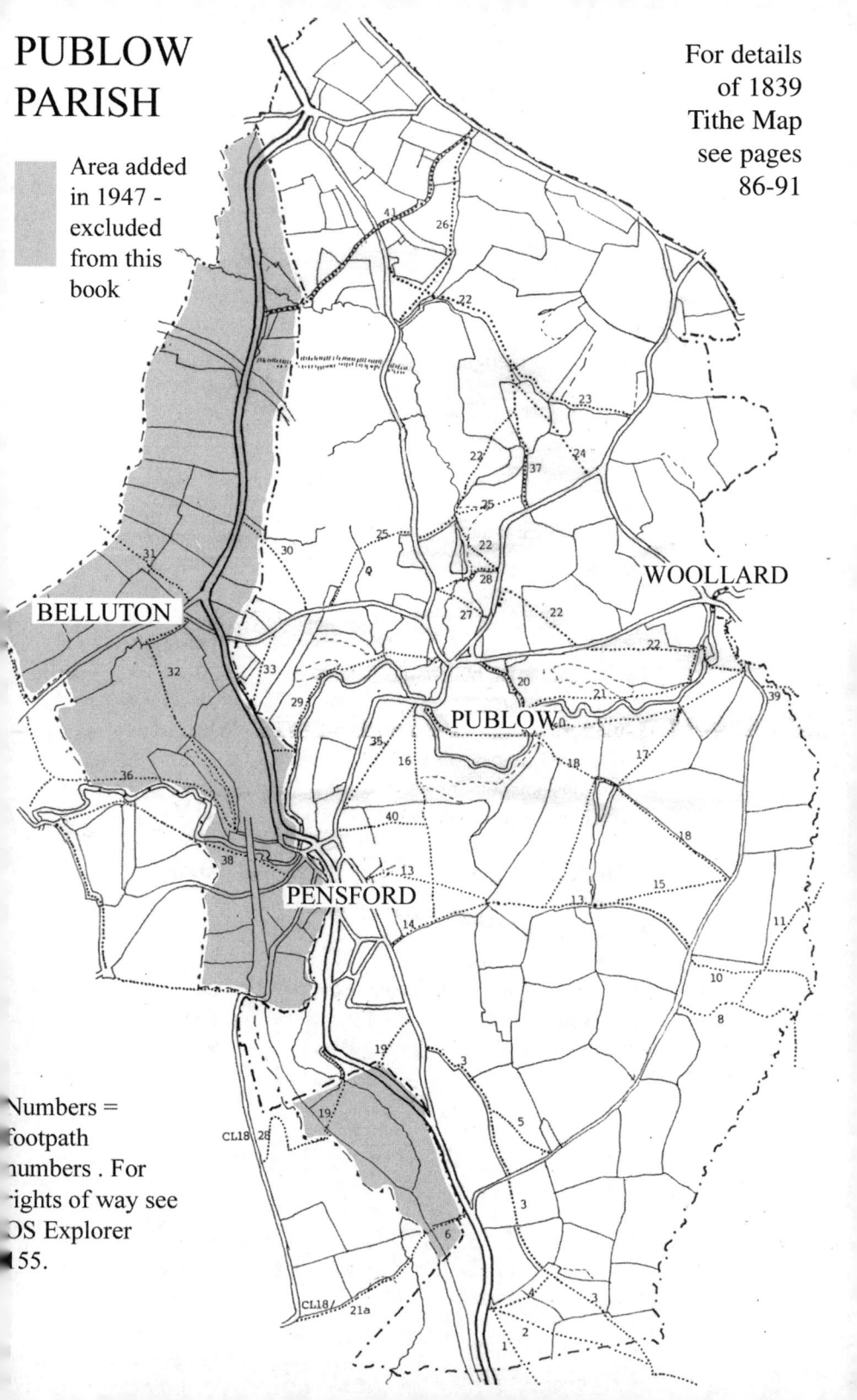

Area added in 1947 - excluded from this book

For details of 1839 Tithe Map see pages 86-91

BELLUTON

WOOLLARD

PUBLOW

PENSFORD

Numbers = footpath numbers. For rights of way see OS Explorer 155.

	Page
Introduction	1
Acknowledgements, 1988	2
Acknowledgements, 2003	3
Illustrations / photographs	3
Ownership of the manors	4
John Locke	7
Place names	8
Field names	10
Topographical names	11
Land use	11
Wildlife	15
The Wansdyke	16
The Hwicce	17
Estate and Parish boundaries	20
Domesday estates	21
Settlements	22
Roads and bridges	26
Commons and coalmines	28
Miscellaneous other themes	30
Gazetteer	**31-78**
References	79
Index of field names	83
Index of surnames in the main text	84
1839 Tithe Map	86-91
Info for visitors	92

Introduction

This history is primarily about places - fields and houses - but inevitably it also tells the story of many of the people and families who have been associated with these places over the centuries. For anyone who wants to explore the many footpaths in the old parish of Publow (which includes most of Pensford and Woollard), much of this history is still observable, or imaginable.

Such exploration on foot offers a fascinating return to the days when a person's parish was pretty much their world. It was far from being the collection of anonymous, boring fields it might appear to be today. A wide variety of topography and semi-natural vegetation could flourish in the age which preceded agricultural mechanisation. The local population's sense of place would be enhanced by shared oral histories and legends relating to all kinds of specific and special areas. This is why place names can be so ancient and so revealing, and this is also why they are considered at some length in the main text, the gazetteer (pages 31-78) place by place.

To help visitors to enjoy such days out exploring, some basic information about local pubs, and pointers to sources for information about transport and accommodation has been added (see page 92). Some of the local footpaths are shown on the map on page iii, but walkers should get the Ordnance Survey Explorer Map 155, which shows all the rights of way, and access to neighbouring parishes.

The text is based on 'Publow Field Names', which was published in 1988. It has been amended, and expanded, and an index of people's names has been added, with references to the properties they owned or leased (for the benefit of family historians).

Note that this book only refers to the old parish of Publow (which excluded part of the modern village of Pensford and the part of Woollard which lies in the parish of Compton Dando). See the map on page iii for an indication of the area of Pensford and Belluton which was transferred from Stanton Drew Parish to Publow Parish in 1947. The modern parish of Publow is 1,723 acres, whereas the overall total for Publow parish as recorded in the 1839 Tithe schedule, the area covered in this book, was 1,397 acres (1,335 acres plus 62 acres of Glebe land). An 1886 survey (see page 13, 'Land Use') put Pensford's area at 323.5 acres - this is the area not covered in the book. The sum of 1,720.5 acres from these two figures seems a fairly good match for the 1,723 quoted above.

The main justification for publishing lies in the excellence of some of the 18th and 19th century sources used, in particular the maps of 1776 and 1806, partial details of which are reproduced here. Ideally these maps would have been repro-

1

duced in full, but the cost would have been prohibitive. Hopefully, one day soon it will be possible to publish good digital copies of all maps in record offices, at affordable prices, for computer access.

The 1839/1840 Tithe Map is also an excellent source, and its numbering sequence has been adopted here for the reference numbers of all the plots (houses or fields) in the main text and gazetteer. Throughout the text the 'T' numbers (eg T7, T85) refer to the plot numbers on the 1839 Tithe Map).

Should anyone want to clear up some of the questions that have not so far been answered, there is still plenty of scope for researching documents at various Record Offices, principally the Somerset Record Office at Taunton, and doing archaeological fieldwork (if you have a few years to spare!). This book has deliberately restricted areas of focus, and is not intended to be a comprehensive history of the area. The content has been organised on a geographical basis, plot by plot, field by field, but the downside of this approach is that much of the material that would otherwise have been linked and grouped thematically or chronologically is dispersed in several places. A few introductory paragraphs listed below cover some of the more general topics, and a few more are added under the final paragraph 'Miscellaneous' by directing the reader to the relevant Tithe numbers in the main text.

Acknowledgements (1988 edition)

Many thanks to Somerset Record Office for permission to reproduce the maps referred to above, for allowing access to various documents, for providing photocopies, and for all the other work which makes such amateur research possible.

Thanks to John Field, Michael Costen and Jennifer Scherr, who all made valuable corrections and additions to an earlier draft of 'Publow Field Names', and to Joe Bettey for most of the extracts from the Publow Court papers, and information about Church Lands (see T136). Thanks to Rob Iles and Mary Stacey for allowing access to Avon County Council's Sites and monuments Record, and to Jennifer Stewart, Michael Ponsford and Vince Russett of Bristol City Museum for identifying pottery finds (see T106).

Any errors or omissions in the final text are, naturally, my fault and not theirs.

Thanks also to the many people who have provided valuable items of information, in particular thanks to Dr Tim Bayley, Barbara Bowes, Keith Clark, Len Coles, Henry Flower, Roy King, Colin Smart, Bill Thompson, and Brian Watson. Above all, thank you to the farmers who have allowed access to their land, and who respect and conserve the ancient features of the local landscape.

Acknowledgments (2003)

Thanks to David Bromwich, John Dallimore, Geoffrey Loxton, Jean Manco, Hannah Lowery, Bob Sydes, and Elizabeth White. It's also worth pointing out that the condition of footpaths and stiles around Pensford and Publow is very much better than when I first started to explore them in 1980, when barbed wire was a fairly common obstruction across rights of way. For this, thanks are largely due to the Ramblers Association and their local representatives over two decades, also to the rights of way sections of Avon County Council until 1994, and its successor Bath and North East Somerset Council (see the photo page 92, a stile and steps installed by B&NES).

Illustrations, photographs and maps

Front cover: Pensford Church by W.W.Wheatley, courtesy of Somerset Archaeological and Natural History Society. Pages 58,59,60: Photographs of Woollard by H.S.Thompson and painting of Woollard by W.W.Wheatley, from Bristol University Library Special Collections Department (refs D.M.85/vol 2/51, D.M.85/vol 2/49a) with the permission of the Director of Information Services, University of Bristol. Pages 16,35,42: English Heritage, aerial photograph RP 108G UK 1661 12JUL46 PR131a/86. Pages 16,42: Ordnance Survey Map 1:2,500, published in 1885. Page 24, from C.Pooley 'Old Stone Crosses of Somerset'. Page 31: photo of Publow Church, 1916, by Miles Farmer. Page 37: drawing of Viaduct View by John Dallimore. Page 39 Painting by E.Parkman, courtesy of Bath Museum. Other maps, courtesy of Somerset Record Office. See references pages 79-82.

Ownership of the manors

Publow and Pensford were two separate manors throughout the medieval era (see below, Domesday estates), although there is frequent confusion caused by the fact that most of Pensford was in the manor of Publow, the more valuable manor. The medieval ownership of the manors of Publow and Pensford is outlined in Collinson's History of Somerset (1791), but unfortunately the details become vague around the middle of the sixteenth century. So it's still unclear how Publow came into the possession of its best known owners, the Popham family. There's no evidence that any of the lords or owners of the manor actually resided in Pensford or Publow, although the Bysses or Bisses (see below) might have done.

Collinson did note how the manor of Publow came to belong to the Hastings family, earls of Huntingdon, but not how or when they disposed of it. He just stated that by 1570, both Publow and Pensford were in the ownership of Sir Henry Becher. As John Bysse had previously bought the manor of Pensford and Belluton in 1562 for £380 [1], Becher probably acquired Pensford from Bysse. A history of the Bisse family suggests that John Bisse had a son and grandson called John Bisse, so the John Bisse buried in Publow in 1622 [2] could be any one of those.

Becher bought the manor of Publow from Henry Hastings, (the Third Earl of Huntingdon, 1536-1595), paying Hasting £1,600 for the manor on 2 June 1565. Becher (c1517-1570) came originally from Bishops Morchard, in Devon. He was Alderman of Broad Street Ward, London in 1570 and Sheriff of London 1569-70.

The 1565 document which recorded this sale of the Manor of Publow is in the Hastings collection at the Huntington Library in San Marino in California. There is probably a good deal of important material relating to 15th and 16th century Publow and Pensford here (see References, page 79). The Somerset Record Office in Taunton has only has a small number of these documents on microfiche, but it does have the Popham archive (DD PO, and DD PO t), the most important collection of documents for the history of Publow. Hastings, whose life is told in a biography by Claire Cross [3], had his main residence in Leicestershire, and spent little time in the west country. He sold at least 65 manors in his lifetime, and one of these was directly to Sir John Popham (1533-1607) - on 18 Apr 1574, the Manor of Langford Leicester, Devon, was sold to J.Popham, M.Smith and A.Ameredith for £1,000. Whether Publow was bought by Sir John Popham (1533-1607) or Sir Francis Popham (1573-1644), and if so how and when, is not known - although there may be documentary records somewhere that will eventually be found to answer that question. The earliest reference to a Popham as Lord of the Manor of Publow so far located is 1637. [4]

The first Popham known to have occupied the nearby Hunstrete House, which was to become the centre of a cluster of parishes owned by the family, was Sir Francis. In his impressive history 'Queen Charlton Perambulation' (1999) [5], G.A.Loxton states that Sir John Popham had acquired Queen Charlton by 1603, and implies this was probably between 1600 and 1603, on the evidence of a lease in the Popham archive at Somerset Record Office. [6] He also states that Popham had already acquired the Hunstrete estate before this date, but he doesn't quote a source for this. Hunstrete was part of the Marksbury estate which had been held by Glastonbury Abbey from the Saxon era until the dissolution of the monasteries instigated by Henry VIII. The gradual process of privatising the immense wealth of the monasteries was one which enriched many lawyers, including Popham.

He had risen to fame (and notoriety) as Lord Chief Justice of England, from 1592 to his death in 1607, but he originally came from Somerset - from Huntworth near North Petherton. Despite his legal and parliamentary career in London (he was first elected MP at the age of 24, representing Lyme Regis) and despite his acquisition of the grand Wiltshire estate of Littlecote, he retained his interest in Somerset. He had built a new mansion (which no longer exists) at Wellington in the last years of his lfe.

In the 1570s and 1580s he had been an MP for Bristol and he was a Somerset Justice of the Peace, as was Henry Hastings' brother Francis. Francis had moved From Leicester to Somerset in 1583, to the manor of North Cadbury, to manage his brother's remaining estates in the south west. Popham also knew Henry Hastings well, to judge from his letter of sympathy to Francis after Henry's death in 1595:

'I can hardly withold myself from tears to enter into the consideration of the loss of so true a servant of God, so loyal and faithful a subject to our most gracious queen and so careful a man of his

Sir John Popham

country's good, and his sovereign's service as your brother hath ever showed himself to have been. I would to God that God in his goodness would yet raise unto her majesty many such.' [7]

These sentiments sound impressive, but then Popham also regarded himself as a friend of William Darrell, who made over the Littlecote Estate to Popham in 1587. This was either a gift, or a payment for legal fees, or, according to a legend popularised in Aubrey's 'Brief Lives', a bribe in return for Justice Popham wrongly acquitting Darrell on a charge of infanticide. It's a grisly story which has been repeated many times, but there appears to be no record to prove it's true.

The Pophams' ownership of the manor in the 17th century seems not have been total, as the 18th and 19th century surveys reveal that about 20 per cent of the land in the parish was owned by other individuals. On the 1776 map, several plots marked 'Sir Charles' referred to ownership by Sir Charles Taint, of the Tynte family which then owned much of Belluton and Pensford (ie the non-Publow part), and extensive estates in the rest of Somerset, see T216, 293 and 294. A sketchy map of Taint's holdings in Publow in 1770 exists at the SRO. In 1769 Edward Popham had sold the Popham's Queen Charlton estate to Vickris Dickinson. [8]

Further research into old deeds might give some idea as to when and how other properties had been sold. The 1839 Tithe Map and apportionment of Publow shows that General Edward William Leyborne Popham (born Leyborne, but he took his mother's surname Popham in 1805) only owned 1,038 of the parish's 1,335 acres. The remaining 297 acres (22 per cent) were owned by 35 landowners, including the Feoffees of Pensford Church Lands (see below). In 1839 John Gales (see T310) was the second largest landowner in the parish, with 99 acres, all in the northern part of Publow. The next largest landowner (excluding James Daubeny's glebe land) was William Lloyd with 33 acres (see T293).

The Pophams, or their Leyborne descendants who took the name Popham, retained the major part of their Somerset estates until sales of 1911, 1917 and the final disposal of Hunstrete House in 1950s.

According to an 1873 return of owners of land, the Pophams owned about 5,600 acres in Somerset (the equivalent of 22 squares on Ordnance Survey map): General Edward William Leyborne Popham of Hunstrete owning 1,517 acres and Francis Leyborne Popham of Littlecote (Wiltshire) owning 4,103 acres in Somerset.

John Locke

The philosopher John Locke (1632-1704) was one of the few Somerset natives who achieved a truly international recognition for their life's work. He was born in Wrington, during a visit to relatives there by his parents who lived in Belluton, about half a mile north of Pensford.

Locke spent his childhood in Belluton, until going to school in London at the age of 14, but he retained links with Pensford and Publow via several properties he owned, and via communications with friends and relations in Pensford, and the area around. Arguably Locke owed everything he achieved later to these local links. Initially it was his father's work for Alexander Popham that led to Locke's acceptance at Westminster School and later Christ Church College, Oxford: necessary paths to acceptance among the nation's elite.

After the death of Locke's father, his namesake John Locke (1606-1661), it was the rent from the land and cottages he then inherited that allowed him to pursue the studies of his choice, rather than take a living as a clergyman (as he had been considering in 1663). The estate was administered for him by his uncle Peter Locke, of Bishop Sutton (1607-1686). The work and life of John Locke is, of course, fascinating and extensively documented, but is outside the scope of this study.

The main reason for including a paragraph about John Locke here is that the wealth of documentation that has survived about the Locke family provides one of the best sources of information about 17th century Pensford and Publow. Much of this is at the Bodleian Library in Oxford.

Various other sources reflect the lives of different members of the Locke family. John Locke's grandfather Nicholas Locke (1574-1648) was a clothier who moved from Dorset to Belluton some time before 1603, when the Pensford cloth industry was still profitable, and amassed the main part of the wealth which came down to his grandson. John Locke Senior (1606-1661) was a lawyer, who was also a clerk to the local Justices of the Peace, and one of his notebooks is at the British Museum (See T91) [9]. It could well contain interesting details about

Pensford and his own work there. Maurice Cranston's biography of Locke [10] states that John Locke Senior's brother, Edward Locke (1610-1663) moved to Bristol in 1635 and 'made a fortune as a brewer'. This seems improbable given the very puritannical ethos of the households of his brother and father, and does not tally with his own role and behaviour as petty constable of Pensford, as recorded in an account of his attempts to control 'riotous' behaviour in Pensford in 1656 (see T86). See also T14.

Place Names

The idea that place names, and surnames, had some original meaning is fairly well understood now, although, sadly, some of the publications which purport to 'define' such names do no such thing. Some writers seem to believe that access to a few old dictionaries and a vivid imagination are good enough qualifications to publish a definitive account. Evidence that this is not the case can probably be found in your local bookshop or library.

The interpretation of place names, which can have elements that are hundreds of years old, can seldom be definitive or certain. There are dozens of known possibilities for all kinds of names, and there could be other possibilities that are not even known about.

To usefully comment on the likelihood of various explanations being right demands extensive knowledge of the evolution of place names in their regional and national contexts. It also requires serious research into the earliest available documentation (which is usually medieval) to find the earliest known versions of those place names. There is no suggestion that this book is based on such expertise, or much direct access to the medieval material, but at least some of the experts have been consulted (see above, acknowledgements) and their advice has been taken on various specifics.

Of course it's possible to even get this wrong - there is one recent publication about a Chew Valley village where the place-name interpretation given by a local expert is wrongly quoted, and the publication from which he is 'quoted' is also wrongly specified.

Place-name study evolves, and some older publications, such as the Rev James Samuel Hill's 'The Place-Names of Somerset' (1914) are now regarded with caution. Hill lived only a few miles away from Pensford, at Stowey. His book, originally written as a series of newspaper articles, was published nine years before the foundation of the English Place-Name Society (1923). Somerset remains the only English county that has not yet been the subject of one of the Society's published studies.

Earlier still, Collinson's 'History of Somerset' (1791) gave the theories of place-name origins which were current then. Regarding the origins of the name Pensford, he quoted William Stukely's statement, that the name is derived from two British words 'pen' and 'isc', signifying 'the head of the river, being near the source of the River Chew'. The minor detail that Pensford is nowhere near the source of the Chew, which is just the other side of Chewton Mendip, has not prevented various later writers from repeating his theory as fact.

The earliest recorded form of the name Pensford is 'Pendelsford', as found on a monumental stone at Keynsham Abbey, thought to date from the 12th century.[11] This casts further doubt on Stukely's suggestion, and any other suggestion that doesn't take account of the 'del' element. Given the possible Mercian origins of the name Publow (see below 'The Hwicce'), it's interesting to note the Mercian name Penda - a Penda was king of Mercia in the early 7th century (see below, in the section on the Wansdyke). Mercia was the the midland kingdom of Anglo Saxon England, which dominated England during the eighth century, and reached as far south as Bath. In 'The Origins of Somerset',[12] Michael Costen suggests that Mercian place name elements reach at least as far south as Kelston (five miles north east of Publow), and that the name Publow could reflect a Mercian settlement within Celtic Somerset. The hard 'k' of Kelston (from Old English 'cealf' - calf) is contrasted with the soft c/ch of Chelwood ('Ceolla's wyrth' - Ceolla's farm). Bath was part of Mercia (or its client kingdom Hwicce, see below) for several centuries, and probably didn't pass into the control of the kings of Wessex until the latter part of King Alfred's reign - the end of the ninth century.

Then again, 'Pen' as a prefix of pre-Saxon Celtic settlements isn't confined to Wales or Cornwall - even Penn in Buckinghamshire is thought to be derived from a Celtic settlement. Either way, there are plenty of other surviving Celtic or Old Welsh (OW) name elements in the vicinity (see below) to corroborate the assumption that the Celts were here and left their mark (perhaps one day DNA profiling will tell us how far their genetic characteristics also survive in the local population).

Penrith, in Cumbria, is interpreted as meaning 'hill ford' or 'chief ford', from 'pen', and 'ritu' (Old Welsh - ford). Margaret Gelling[13] says 'pen' is one of the commonest Celtic place names in the English landscape 'but its true frequency is difficult to assess because it is impossible to distinguish from OE 'penn' - pen for animals'. In her later book 'The Landscape of Place-Names' (2000) she duly notes Pensford as 'either OE penn 'enclosure' or British hill name 'Pen'', plus - ford.[14] Neither versions properly explain 'Pendelsford', though.

Regarding the 'ford' element, the character of the River Chew in pre-medieval times would have been very different to today's channelled, reduced flow. It would have been wider, but intermittently fordable - even the Avon had an ancient ford below the Clifton hill forts - it was finally blown up in 1883 to make the channel easier for shipping. Early fords were sometimes supplemented with planks or boards.

Field Names

The fact that fields have names is less well known. Like the names of settlements, field names can also be hundreds of years old, having been verbally passed from generation to generation long after the original meaning of the name has been forgotten.

Saxon words form elements in many field names in Somerset and Avon, and although not all will necessarily be survivals from pre-Norman times, others probably are. Some names, such as that of the River Chew, are thought to be relics of the Celtic culture which preceded the Saxons. Other names possibly surviving from that era are Priest Down (from 'prisc', Old Welsh for a copse or thicket - see T274), and Candlestick Brook (from 'canto', OW for an edge, but from which similar derivatives have been applied elsewhere to boundaries).

The surviving Saxon or Old English elements in field names would not have referred to fields as we now see them. Some names just denote woodland, or the clearance of woodland. For example, names ending in -ley (OE 'leah') may denote clearances made in woodland in or by the Saxon era.

According to Margaret Gelling, "this is by far the commonest topographical term in English place-names, but its poor showing in names recorded before A.D. 730 establishes that it was not much used in the early Anglo Saxon period ... it indicates areas which were well wooded in the middle Saxon period." However, by the late Saxon period, 'leah' was losing its assocattion with woodland and developing a meaning 'pasture'. [15] Local names of this type include Hursley / Usley (see T361), Catley / Oatley (see T108), Whitley (see T151) and a group around The Ley / Lye / Leigh (see T122, 133, 130, 126 etc). Names denoting smaller patches of woodland include several 'grove' names stretching across the middle of the parish (T111, 127, 129, 131, 215, 218, 303).

The fields of Publow parish began to look like modern fields from about the 16th century when systems of communal use of land increasingly gave way to private use of land, the private lands being enclosed with new hedges. The history of hedges after 1776 is mostly one of their removal. Speculation as to how all this might have happened forms the main part of the following text, but it should not be regarded as much more than a preliminary investigation: as I've already admitted, much of the older documentary evidence, which may contain crucial earlier forms of names, has not so far been checked. Also, there has been very little archaeological fieldwork.

Topographical Names

Recent work in place name studies, particularly that by Margaret Gelling and Ann Cole, has shown that the topographical significance of early place name elements was far more subtle and specific than earlier studies recognised. The following categories of name elements in local names roughly follows those used by Gelling and Cole in their 'The Landscape of Place-Names' (2000), which can be referred to for a detailed analysis of the nuances of various topographical terms in other English contexts.

Some of the following fields have had alternative names which imply contradictory topographical references, but that's only to be expected with the mutation of names over centuries.

- Rivers, springs, and ponds. T103 etc (Alderwells), T134 (Beadons), T301, T350 (Carsbrook), T209 (Ware Pool), T152.
- Marsh, moor and floodplain. T14, T15, T219, T220 etc (Ham), T308 (Hawkham), T11 etc (Markham), T58 (Sideham).
- Valleys, hollows and remote places. T350 (Amercombe), T379 (Babyland), T134 (Bitham), T14 (Marcombe).
- Hills, slopes and ridges. T200 etc (Bookhill), T316 (Borough Bank), T45a (Pensford Down), T58 (Sidon).
- Woods and clearings. T130 etc (Birchwood), Catley (T108), T11, T127, T129, T303 etc (Grove), T172 (Herns), T361 etc (Hursley), T122 (Leigh), T173 (Lords Wood), T110 etc (Lye), T126 etc (Lydown), T115 (Lyfield), T215 etc (Seagrove), T361 etc (Usley), T154 (Wethergroves), T150, T151 (Whitley).
- Ploughland, meadow and pasture. T379 (Babyland), T12, T11 etc (Butts), T5 (Butts Meadow), T214, T370, T392 etc (Charlton Field), T136 etc (Church Lands), T327 etc (Cuckow Sleight), T357, T359 (Gunder Mead), T268 (Hedge Mead), T118 (Home Meads), T115 (Lyfield), T154 etc (Mill Mead), T126 (Pool Mead), Starve Acre (T399), T194 (Stout's Mead), T195 (Walls Mead).

Land Use

700 to 900 AD
The article written by Michael Costen for 'The Natural History of the Chew Valley' (1987) [16] is worth quoting at length:

'It seems likely that this is the period of consolidation of settlement by the Anglo-Saxons. However, they had taken over, and were exploiting a landscape in which the major manmade features had long since been determined and in which the pattern of estates was already settled. The area was almost certainly well exploited by 700 and most of the place-names which we see today were already in use. Although further place-names were added in the 8th and the 9th centuries, those names which are descriptive of the landscape and of land use were probably the earliest. It is important to realise that most of the names of villages and hamlets which we still have are the names of estates and not the names of groups of houses and their dense distribution across the landscape means that the Chew Valley was well settled from an early date ... Little can be said about agriculture in the area, though evidence of other place-names nearby suggests that the open-field system had not yet developed and that farming was probably carried on by the intensive exploitation of small farm units combined with the extensive use of pasture areas.'

1086 AD

More specific written evidence becomes available with the Domesday report of 1086, which specified the numbers of animals, and such things as the area of woodland and pasture. Unfortunately it didn't mention Pensford or Publow, and only gave data for Belluton, which may or may not have corresponded to Publow. In 'The Natural History of the Chew Valley', the formulae quoted by Oliver Rackham [17] were used to estimate acreages for Belluton: arable - 480 acres, wood - 56 acres, permanent pasture - 24 acres, meadow (ie mown for hay etc) - 32.4 acres (total 592 acres). As suggested below (see 'Domesday Estates') this does not appear to equate to the 1,723 acres of the modern parish of Publow. 47 sheep were recorded, which is a clue to the under-recording of pasture, insofar as sheep might be expected to need at least an acre each. But as the record stands, pasture and meadow appear to have accounted for just under 10 per cent of local land use in 1086, while arable was an amazing 81 per cent.

Michael Costen notes: 'Probably most agriculture was carried on in quite small units so that as open field agriculture developed, it did so in quite small areas and not in the very large fields of popular imagination. However, this period is noted for its wide extension of ploughland and even in 1086 arable cultivation was the dominant feature of agricultural practice and remained so for about two centuries.'

1300 to 1800 AD

Michael Costen again, writing of the period 1300 to 1500: 'From the beginning of the 14th century, the decline in population and the consequent change in agricultural practice led to changes in the landscape. The major difference was that the amount of land under the plough began to decline. Instead, much land was given over to permanent pasture. This pasture was adapted to feed sheep and cattle and, especially where cattle were raised, this led to the enclosure of the pasture into what we now call fields, but contemporaries mostly referred to as closes. There had always been some closes around villages and hamlets, names such as innicks or ennox indicating closes permanently enclosed and usually used for crops. The innovation was that these fields were often found scattered inside the old open fields. Some ploughing did go on and where that was the case it was still normal for grain to be grown in the open fields, now much shrunken. Aerial photography reveals the extent of this shrinkage in ploughland as relict ridge and furrow ... Shrunken villages and hamlets are part and parcel of this change, although this is not the only period in which settlements shrank or were deserted.'

The sixteenth and 17th centuries saw continuing use of the arable lands in strips, and those on Publow Hill (T314 across to 334) were still in use in 1839. But there was also ongoing enclosure, with increasing acreages being put under grass, and all the common land shown on the 1776 map had been enclosed and privatised by 1839 (see below Commons and Coalmines). Other reverse 'S' shaped relics of medieval ploughed furlongs (egT359, T139 and perhaps T151) may be relics of other smaller areas of open field.

1800 to 2000

Some field books maintained by the Popham estate give data on quite a wide range of crops, and how they were rotated in specific fields. The sequence for T358 from 1828 to 1844 is quoted in the gazetteer section, as an example.

In 1866 there was the first of the agricultural census series that evolved into those annually compiled by the former Ministry of Agriculture Fisheries and Food (MAFF).[18] Returns for each parish in England were instituted for numbers of animals and acreages of different crops, or land use. Surprisingly for such a recent document, even even with the 1866 data it is difficult to be sure about the exact areas being recorded, as different 'parish' units were specified in the animal and cropping returns. The land use returns are for Pensford and Publow, but the farm animal returns are for Belluton and Publow. The most obvious conclusion is that the names Belluton and Pensford were used as alternatives for the same area, but it's hard to be certain about that.

The land use returns gave a total area of 323.5 acres for Pensford, which probably included Belluton. In Publow, 881.75 acres were accounted for, so the overall agricultural total was 1205.25 acres. Note that woodland and waste was not recorded in those totals, so the overall land area was more than this (see the Introduction for notes on overall acreages). Of those 1205.25 acres, the following totals were recorded for 1866: wheat 54.75, barley 57, oats 40.5, rye 0, beans 27, peas 11, potatoes 49, turnip & swede 41.5, mangold 7, carrots 0, cabbage, kohlrabi & rape 2.5, hops 0, vetches & lucerne 0.75, clover etc in rotation

105.25, bare & fallow 47, permanent pasture 761.75. So grassland (to include clovers etc with pasture) had risen to 72 per cent of the recorded area. The animals which would have grazed this are recorded under different place names, but possibly the same area (see above): Belluton and Publow.

	milk cows	cattle age >2	cattle age<2	sheep age>1	sheep age<1	pigs
Belluton	25	3	11	102	36	101
Publow	119	77	62	304	166	107

None of this mentions the orchards that were a feature of Somerset from at least the 18th century and probably much earlier. In 1791 Collinson decried Pensford as 'pleasantly situated in a fine woody vale, almost surrounded with small hills, well cultivated, and having on their sides several hanging orchards, which form a pleasing rural scene from every part of the town'. The Tithe schedule records large areas of orchard around the settlements, and the 1885 Ordnance Survey maps confirm this. The orchards may have just been recorded as permanent pasture in 1866, as all of them were probably intermittently grazed. Nearly all of the old orchards had been grubbed up by 2000.

In 1945 the proportion of the area under grass in the Chew Valley area was said to be about 65 per cent, rising to about 90 per cent by 1955. By 2000 not much ancient pasture had survived the dual threats of replacement by rye grass, or encroaching scrub where grazing stopped.

A young oak planted in 1983, pictured in 1987 and 2003

Wildlife

Wild cats: see T108 (Catley).
Deer: see T387 (Lypeat).
Rabbits: see T45a, T125, T132, T140, T210 (Conygre)
Wildflowers: In 1984 a leaflet titled 'Pensford Flora' was published, based on one year's botanical surveying of 20 square kilometres (4,940 acres) of the parish and the area around it. About 420 species found growing naturally in the area and the data was, with a few corrections and additions, incorporated into 'The Flora of the Bristol Region' (2000). Several botanical records for Pensford and Publow were published by J.W.White in 1912 [19] and are quoted re T58, T102, T173, T343, T364, with updated observations. Other species are mentioned ref T207, T218, T238, T274, T308 etc.

Trees: all of the early maps, and even early aerial photographs (1946), show how full of trees the hedges and fields were. This was partly the inheritance of careful management by the Popham Estate, and their timber surveys showed the value they placed on non-woodland timber. Some particularly fine old oaks were noted and measured in 1986 for 'The Natural History of the Chew Valley' (1987). Finest of these old oaks was the Publow Oak, see T281. Two other notable old trees were at T96 and T59.

J.W.White

For further references to trees, see T103, T104 and T109 (Alderwells), T130 etc (Birchwood), T200 etc (Bookhill), T114 (Crabtree Close), T116 (Hollybushes). It's never too late to plant more - in 1983 eight or so young oak trees (and an alder, a couple of beech and a small-leaved lime) were planted around the parish by Chew Valley Friends of the Earth, with grant aid from Wansdyke Council. The trees are all doing well twenty years later (see the photographs opposite), apart from one of the two at the top of Pensford Hill, which was knocked down by a verge-trimmer.

Hedges: are mentioned throughout the text. The earlier sections on land use outline the development of hedges and enclosures, but the process of hedgerow removal was already under way by 1839, as is evident in comparisons of the

1776 and 1839 maps. Pre- and post-1776 hedges can usually be identified from the map of that date. It might be interesting to do a survey using 'species per length of hedge' dating techniques, but preliminary investigations suggested a degree of unreliability that might not justify the amount of time and effort they can take. The general rule 'straight line=boring (recent), wiggly line = interesting (older)' may not be very scientific, but appeared to be about as useful, taken in conjunction with the bank and ditch profiles and general visual impression.

Woodland: see T173 (Lords Wood), T105 (Publow Wood), T218. (Seagrove Brake) etc. T182 is plantation now but was pasture in 1839. See also 'Grove' names at T111, 127, 129, 131, 215, 218, 303.

The Wansdyke

The oldest artificial boundary in the parish is probably the Wansdyke, which runs across from T350 and T362, bearing no relation to present boundaries.

No one knows for sure exactly when or why it was built. As Costen says: 'Anyone attempting to write the history of the period from 407 to the end of the Celtic, that is Old Welsh, Somerset in the mid-seventh century is faced with the near insuperable problem that we have no written sources. Such accounts as we have ... are fragmentary and of dubious quality.' [12]

So, there are many different theories about the Wansdyke, with various phases of struggles between Celts and Saxons being the most favoured eras. -An earthwork of this antiquity could well have had different significances and associated activity in different phases, and opposing theories will doubtless continue to be argued about indefinitely, and inconclusively. The archaeological surveys of the 1990s yielded interesting data regarding the excavation of sections of the Wansdyke, including digs at T348/T350, and a major conclusion is that the structure here and in other local stretches of the Wansdyke closely resembled the plan

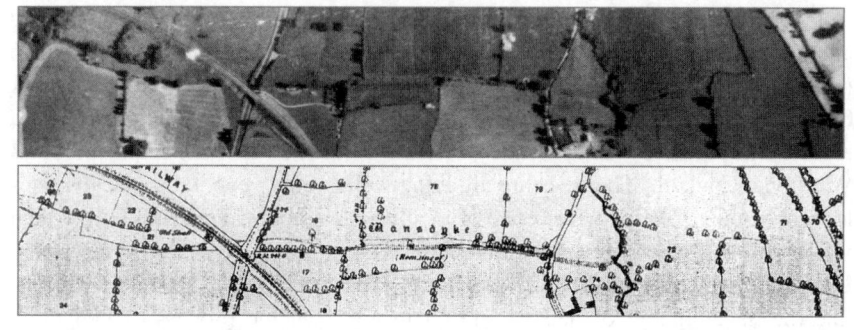

The Wansdyke just north of Publow from the air, 1946, compared with the OS map of 1885

Excavations on the Wansdyke, by T348, in 1995

of Roman dykes. This suggests the possibility of a mid-fifth century date for the initial building. Theories which had previously been given some credence included those of Fox and Fox, who in 1960 suggested that West Wansdyke was likely to be a West-Saxon construction, 'on a line imposed by Penda of Mercia after AD 628'. Some of the alternative suggestions are discussed by Keith Gardner in 'Bristol and Avon Archaeology 1998': he says the date of Wansdyke's construction may relate either to the period before the Battle of Badon, (C. AD 485 +/-) or to that following the Saxon capture of Gloucestershire and Bath in AD 577, after the battle of Dyrham. [20]

The Hwicce

The Wansdyke has also been discussed in relation to the early Saxon kingdom of the Hwicce (to the north of the Wansdyke) and even the regional kingdoms that preceded the Roman invasion - the Romans adopted the existing regional tribal groupings as the basis for their civitates, and these may also have survived the Roman exit from Britain around AD 409.

Some of the more interesting theories about the Hwicce have been summarised recently by Jean Manco. [21] Before the Romans arrived, the area between the River Avon and the Mendips had formed the approximate boundary between the territories of the Dobunni, of the area in and around Gloucestershire, and the

Durotriges to the south. This division may have survived after the Romans left, and it has been pointed out that the Dobunni territory looks very similar to the old diocese of Worcester, which had been created for the Anglo-Saxon kingdom of the Hwicce. This diocese had the River Avon as its southern boundary, but the territory of the Dobunni, in the opinion of Barry Cunliffe extended some way further south, to the Mendips. [22]

The Wansdyke is between these two frontiers and could relate to a mid-fifth century response to attempts by the Britons to demarcate their surviving land in the south west: Nicholas Higham has suggested that the Saxon incursions into England after 409 were so swift and successful that they achieved control over most of lowland England by 441 and could impose treaty terms that gave them most of the east, and left the west to the Britons. [23] The Hwicce could have been a British buffer zone, surviving by tributes to the Saxons to the east. That arrangement appears to have ended around 628 when King Penda of Mercia defeated the Hwicce, and the kingdom became a client kingdom of Mercia. It was not fully absorbed into Mercia until about 790, possibly on the death of their last king. The Wansdyke's bank and ditch face north, which obviously supports the general assumption that it was constructed by the people on the south side.

Jean Manco suggests that for the British, trying to defend their south western territories in the mid fifth century 'on the north their best strategy would be a defensive line along the hills overlooking the Bristol Avon and the Kennet.' However, although the old hillforts of Maes Knoll and Stantonbury overlook the Avon, the route chosen for the Wansdyke between the two clearly did not - the route is too far to the south, and there is one large gap. The famous 'Publow Gap' is the missing link in the west Wansdyke. There is no trace of the Wansdyke between T302 and Compton Dando, and the beginning of the gap can be seen from the aerial photo and 1885 map on page 16.

The gap has been variously explained, but none of the explanations are very convincing. If the Wansdyke was a token boundary rather than a strictly defensive one, it may simply be that the brook flowing from the north down to Publow and the river Chew from Publow to Compton Dando formed an adequate demarcation.

Like Offa's Dyke, the Wansdyke is badly situated from a defensive point of view, [24] and so maybe the people south of the Wansdyke were not allowed the option of siting the line of the Wansdyke where they would have ideally wanted it. The line of the Wansdyke as an agreed boundary would make sense as a line determined by a more powerful group to the north, which wanted to ensure that it retained the lands around Publow Hill, and the Hick Mead, etc. It's also possible that the Wansdyke may have overlain existing estate boundaries, and lands either side of the dyke could have been utilised by the same people or estate.

Michael Costen has shown how this appears to have been the case in Stanton Prior, a few miles away. Using the evidence of Saxon Charters he suggested that the Saxon estates of Stanton Prior, Marksbury, Corston and Priston had boundaries which were very similar to those of the modern parishes, and that all could have been considerably older than the Wansdyke. [25]

It may be stretching a point to suggest this, but there are a number of otherwise unexplained names featuring 'Hick','Hicks' and 'Hix' right across the plateau where the Publow gap exists (see T326 etc). There are further such place names in Compton Dando (Hick Meadow and Hick's Lay) and Keynsham (Hick's Gate). The obvious assumption is that these names would be derived from a surname, as a few Hicks surnames have been recorded locally.

However, those references have not been linked to these fields specifically, and the extent of the area covered by the Hick/Hix field names, and the several variations in the spelling, seem atypical of such tenant or owner field names, suggesting an early origin of some sort. As a remote possibility, could the name be an ancient derivation from Hwicce? Maybe not, as the pronuncation of Hwicce is generally taken to be something like Wych (as in Wychwood). On the other hand, there are examples of 'ch' and 'k' sounds mutating, and the Mercian pronunciation of 'c' was 'k', as noted above with reference to Kelston.

The 1839 Tithe map shows that a block of about 100 acres in Publow north of the Wansdyke was in one non-Popham ownership, that of John Gale (see above). The Wansdyke forms the southern boundary of this block, at T347, and it's tempting to speculate about the possibility of this northern part of the parish correlating to a later Saxon estate based on Charlton and extending to the Wansdyke. On the other hand it could just be that Edward Popham sold off the northern part of Publow when he sold his Queen Charlton land (see T310) in 1769. Still, as the 1776 survey, 1806 map and 1911 map show, the Pophams did retain numerous plots in Queen Charlton parish.

In agreeing with Collinson that the name Publow might be derived from the burial mound (-hlaew = low = tumulus)(see T316) of some person (Pybba- = Pub-), Costen suggested that maybe Pybba was a leader connected with the construction of the dyke. [26] It has subsequently been pointed out that Pybba was a personal name popular in Mercia in the early seventh century. [27] Although this doesn't necessarily imply the name was not in use elsewhere, perhaps Pybba, if he existed, was connected with determining the line of the Wansdyke rather than constructing it.

Estate and Parish Boundaries

Unfortunately no such Saxon charters have survived for the Publow area, and the absence of entries for Pensford and Publow in Domesday poses further questions (see below).

The earliest known definition of the boundary of the manor of Publow is dated 1671 and reads:

'It beginneth at a certain place called ye Lypiatt ... [illegible word] .. betweene ye parishes of Charlton and Publow and so extendeth itself Eastward leading towards Woollards Hill along a highway there. and thence downe to Woollards bridge southward and thence to a place called ley in ye parish of Publow and thence it extendeth itself southward to a place called Pryors hill and soe along the highway leading to Pensford Townes end, to an antient pound called ye lord's pound. soe along ye backside of ye towne unto ... [small hole in document] ... called horne lane unto Pensford Bridge and so along downe ye River northeastward until wee come to Publow church and thence to a Tenement of land called Farmer Cages in this parish, and thence up to a place called Ursley Hill northwestward to the road way leading to Bristol. thence to a place called Short lane end, and soe eastward to ye place called Lypiatt where we first began.' [28]

This account is interesting, but disappointingly vague about the precise boundaries. The first clear picture comes with the 1776 map 'A Survey of the Manors of Pensford, Publow and Woollard, the property of Edward Popham Esq'. The boundaries shown in this are repeated with only minor changes in maps up to 1947.

So, the boundaries shown here stayed fairly stable, but their origins my not have been contemporary with each other. The brook flowing north to Woollard is probably an ancient boundary (see above). But the rectangular chunk in the south west looks like it originated on a drawing board, perhaps in the 17th or 18th centuries. Probably the land from T58 (Sideham Common) extended down to T150 as one area of rough grazing shared as a common with Stanton Drew - inter-commoning had been a fairly widespread custom. [29] A deal was probably made between the respective lords of the manor. This rectangular intrusion obscures the fact that a previous, possibly ancient, boundary may have existed in Salters Brook. This remained as the boundary from Sideham northwards to the Chew.

The 'antient pound' could have been near where T116 adjoins T75 and T74, but (see the accounts of T45a and T116 for the clues) could have been at the southern end of T116, where it adjoins Stanton Drew parish. This would make more sense as a boundary marker, and would tie in with a 1763 reference to 'The

Old Way' (see 45a). Horne Lane was probably what is now known as Policeman's Lane, extending down to and across Salter's Brook at that time.

The boundaries to the north and west also look odd and non-ancient. T12, T288 and T289 are called Butts, and these originate in the arable open field system of Belluton, from which they have been separated by the boundary. Similarly, further north, T359 looks like part of a possible field system stretching westwards but overlain by the boundary.

The northern boundary is not very clearly shown in the 1776 map, but a map of 1806 suggests some integration of arable lands with Queen Charlton parish. There seems to have been a lot of open field cultivation on this plateau, presumably a continuation of the 'champayn' fields noted by Leyland in the 1540s, see T392 etc. [30]

The north east boundary follows the road to T408, where it meets a rectangular incursion of Compton Dando. This shape is also shown on a map of Compton Dando dated 1755. Then at the northern edge of T242 a brook runs down to the Chew and the boundary follows this. Again, a possible ancient boundary.

Publow parish's boundary running south from Woollard is Candlestick Brook, and as noted earlier, Michael Costen has suggested that this could be derived from 'canto', OW for an edge, or boundary.

On the western boundary of Publow is Marcombe (T14), which could be derived from the OE for a boundary, plus 'combe'. There is a similar example at Bathampton where a 'Mercombe' is on that parish's boundary with Marshfield.[31] In some counties '-combe' has been noted as particularly applying to short, shallow, wide side valleys [13] and that could be the case with local examples, such as Marcombe (T14) and Amercombe (T294/T350).

Pensford's marketplace's function as a local centre for punishment in the 17th century is noted in T91, but the parish boundary also contains two grimmer reminders of medieval punishment: Gibbett Lane to the north (see T361) and Gallows Close (T153) to the south. Both sites would have been chosen for their highly visible locations, for maximum deterrent effect. There doesn't appear to be much evidence of how, how often, or when their respective gibbet or gallows were in use.

Domesday Estates

The absence of Publow and Pensford from Domesday (though Woollard may be represented by Wulfward's half hide and half plough - about 60 acres - in Keynsham Manor) poses two questions. On the assumption that Publow wasn't simply omitted or regarded as waste, 1) which estates did include Publow and where were the boundaries? 2) when were they rearranged?

Six surrounding estates are mentioned in Domesday: Keynsham, Stanton Drew, Chelwood, Compton Dando, Belluton and Norton Malreward. Estimates of the Domesday acreages of these parishes has been compared with the acreages of the modern parishes ('The Natural History of the Chew Valley' page 65) and for several parishes, including Stanton Drew, Chelwood and Compton Dando, there is a striking ratio of 1:2. The boundaries of these parishes also suggest stability and possible continuity from Norman and pre-Norman estates. However, a 1:2 projection of Belluton's estimated acreage in AD 1086 (592 acres) would give 1,184 acres - not very similar to that of the modern Publow (1,723 acres). Norton Malreward's acreage seems to have drastically decreased, possibly largely included in the modern parish of Whitchurch. (Queen) Charlton was also not included in Domesday, being included in Keynsham, but the name implies the possibility of a Saxon estate based on Charlton, possibly extending to the Wansdyke - see T347. Most of the major local settlements at that time have -ton suffixes: Belluton, Norton, Stanton, Compton, Charlton, Clutton, Sutton, etc.

None of this answers the two questions above. Without advancing good evidence to support this suggestion, perhaps the major part of Publow was counted under Belluton's lands, a part in the east under Wulfward's, and a part in the north east of Publow as an unspecified part of Keynsham corresponding to an old estate of Charlton. All could have been within the territory of Keynsham and might have been rationalised by Keynsham Abbey in the 13th or 14th centuries: see below.

Settlements

The fact that Pensford and Publow are not mentioned in Domesday does not of course necessarily mean there was absolutely no settlement there at that time, or that there was none before 1086. There could have been all sorts of site occupations and land use in the Bronze Age, Iron Age, Roman era, etc, which disappeared without trace, or at least without leaving any evidence that has so far been noticed or recognised. However, remains of Saxon occupation have survived in the names noted above, the -ley and 'leigh' names being likely to have had Anglo Saxon farmsteads or hamlets and territories associated with them.

The field pattern south of Belluton, with its classic reverse 's' shaped furlongs, confirms the Domesday record of Belluton as the focus of later settlement to a nucleated village with extensive open fields. The strips on the hill around T329 were probably used as strips in an open field from the 16th to 18th centuries, but do not seem comparable to those at Belluton. The name 'Winyards' survives for many of these strips, see T313 and 318, and suggests that the whole block might have been laid out as a vineyard by Keynsham Abbey. Before or after the dissolution of Keynsham Abbey (1539) the land was probably converted to open field system, using the still visible strips across the gradient. The original labour force for the vineyard might have been seasonally housed in buildings at T316 and 410 (see below), which might explain the distance of the field from a major settlement. No archaeological evidence has been found (or sought, yet) to support this suggestion.

It's generally assumed that Publow is a village which must have shrunk from its original size in the medieval era, but few suggestions have been made as to the extent or location of that settlement. Again, this could be a task for a future survey, looking carefully for evidence on the ground. Note that one cluster of buildings which has now disappeared is shown on the 1776 map - in and around T272. Whitley Batts is another hamlet which could be medieval or earlier.

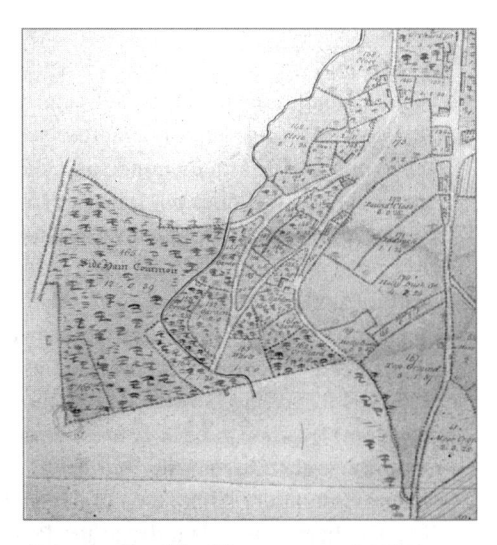

Pensford's old village green (T45a), and Sideham Common (T58), in 1806

Pensford retains at least two distinct ancient centres of development. There is T45a, a village green showing a typical group of dwellings around an area extending from common land etc (see T58 etc), and the market area (see below, and T91).

It is likely that Keynsham Abbey was responsible for the development of Pensford as a market town. The Abbey, founded around 1170, had obtained licenses for the markets at Marshfield in 1256, and at Keynsham in 1307. [32] The Abbey may also have seen the potential of Pensford, sited on an increasingly busy thoroughfare. Pensford is not mentioned in the Nomina Villarum (1315-16) or the Exchequer Lay Subsidies of 1327 (although Publow is) [33] so Pensford's development probably began some time after this. The absence of any known charter granting Pensford its market does not of course mean the market was necessarily unauthorised. Sir William Savage's history of Somerset towns admits the probability of unknown charters. The Black Death of 1348-1350 is in roughly the same time frame, and could have also been associated with the decline of Publow and the growth of Pensford. There is little data on how the Black Death affected Somerset, but G.A.J.Loxton quotes a manor roll for Ston Easton, a few miles south of Publow, which records that 12 of the 16 tenants there died in

1348.[5] Publow is about midway between there and Bristol where 'almost the whole strength of the town died', and so could well have suffered a similar fate.

There is a fragment of sculpture set into the wall of a cottage at the back of the Miners Welfare Institute, and this could have come from the top of a medieval cross. It does not figure in Charles Pooley's 'The Old Stone Crosses of Somerset' (1887), presumably because no-one had recognise it. [34] The book described over 200 stone crosses, many of which had been destroyed in the 17th century, and many of which were relatively simple wayside crosses at crossroads or in churchyards. A smaller number had more elaborate heads on the crosses, and the three pictured here are examples. All three survived because they were removed to private houses. Pooley thought the Harptree cross (now in Taunton Museum) was late twelfth or early thirteenth century, whereas the Ditcheat cross could have dated from the fourteenth century, or more specifically from 1332, when Glastonbury Abbey was granted a licence for a market and fair at Ditcheat. The Ditcheat cross is similar to the Pensford cross, and there could be a similar background and date, with the possibility of Keynsham Abbey securing a licence for a market at Pensford not long after this. The importance of the cross was not just religious - Pooley noted of the crosses which stood at the centre of village market- places 'The market tolls which were paid at these crosses went mostly to increase the revenues of certain religious houses, and it was to promote the payment of this tax, as well as to advance the cause of religion, that preaching

The heads of the crosses from Pensford (left), Ditcheat (right) and Harptree (opposite)

friars frequently addressed the people on market and fair days at the cross.' For more about the history of Pensford's market, and its importance in the surrounding area, see T91.

Regarding the later growth of Pensford, Savage noted it as 'a good example of cloth workers migrating into villages with water power to escape the restrictions of the town guilds'. [35] By 1540 Leland was able to describe Pensford as a 'small but ancient' market town. One indication of its status in the early 17th century is a map of Great Britain by Guiljelmus Blaew (1571-1638) which shows only five towns in North Somerset: Bristol, Bath, Axbridge, Wells and Pensford (see page ii). Somerset's Quarter Sessions were held at Taunton, Ilchester, Bridgwater and Wells, and in the early 17th century Pensford appears to have been one of the centres for the divisions within that circuit, as there is a reference to Petty Sessions held at Pensford in 1612. [36] Petty Sessions at that time were for administrative purposes only, for such matters as regulating public houses. The legend that the savage Lord Chief Justice Jeffreys tried rebels in Pensford after the 1685 Monmouth Campaign is not right - the 'Bloody Assize' hearings were at Taunton and Wells. However, many local men were among the hundreds hanged or transported, as is well documented elsewhere.

The textile industry in Pensford seems to have just about survived to the early part of the the 18th century. Daniel Defoe, in his 'Tour Through Great Britain' probably came through Pensford in the 1720s, and he noted that it was was one of the half dozen or so Somerset towns producing 'Spanish medleys'. This industry, small scale as it may well have been, must have virtually all gone in the next 60 years according to Collinson's remark in 'History of Somerset' (1791), that Pensford 'has dreadfully decayed since that time [the 16th century] and now, bereft of the benefit of trade, many of the houses are fallen into ruins'. Most towns of similar importance to Pensford in the 16th century still have numerous fine and substantial buildings from that time. The question as to why this is not the case in Pensford is one which has not really been addressed. A possible clue as to a specific cause for the 'decay' noted by Collinson comes from some early 17th century Somerset Quarter Sessions records. From 1616 to 1634 there are records of various villages in the surrounding area (including Saltford, Stanton Drew, Queen Charlton and Brislington) having to pay a levy for the 'poor of Pensford'. The Sessions hearings were to hear to the objections of those villages to continued payment of the levy, so presumably it had been in force for some time before then. [106]

This levy is reputed to have beome necessary after a disastrous epidemic struck Pensford, but I have not been able to locate a source to confirm this, or give any details of cause and effect, or the mechanism by which such a levy was imposed (presumably by the Somerset Justices of the Peace). The implication of such a levy must be that many people might have died or been disabled or orphaned by the epidemic, and it has been suggested that this epidemic probably occurred in the late 1590s. [108] Either the epidemic did not spread to neighbouring villages, or Pensford was worse affected than other villages because it was already in a state of relative poverty or decline. There had been food shortages in the 1590s, and outbreaks of plague locally in that decade and the next . Then again, perhaps the disease was something like anthrax, which became known as wool-sorter's disease in the 19th century, but was known as 'black bane' in 16th and 17th century epidemics. It was associated with the activities of two industries which were both local specialities - with handling wool (ref the clothing industry) or hides (ref the tanning industry). Whatever the nature of the epidemic, it would not have been good for business!

Roads and Bridges

Pensford's reputation as a 'great thoroughfare' in the 17th century [37] suggests that the Pensford route from Wells to Bristol may have already become more significant than the Chew Stoke route, which might have been more used in the medieval period.

If so, Pensford's ascendancy might have partly resulted from 12th and 13th century clearances of forest to the north in Fillwood Chase (see T387), and from the replacement of Pensford's ford with a bridge. Chew Magna's Tun Bridge is thought to date from the late 15th century, but the Stanton Drew bridge and Pensford's may be earlier in origin (while Publow bridge may be 18th century and the now replaced Woollard bridge perhaps early 16th century). [38] Of course these approximate dates give no clue as to the dates of possible earlier bridges. Bearing in mind the possible role of Keynsham Abbey in promoting Pensford as a market town, it is not impossible that the Abbey also played a part in planning the lay-out of the market area. This in turn could have involved diverting the tracks that may have existed previously, as suggested by the map on page 27. On the assumption that the church or chapel at Pensford had already been constructed on its present site, the new street might have been deliberately aligned towards it (that line may not be particularly striking now, but then most of the buildings either side of the street now are 18th or 19th century, not necessarily observing precisely the plots occupied by former dwellings). A similar alignment of a short street on the church occurs at Publow. The map of 1776 also strongly suggests the remains of a similar arrangement of dwelling plots laid out either side of this street, with the 1839 map showing a gradually continuing erosion of that pattern.

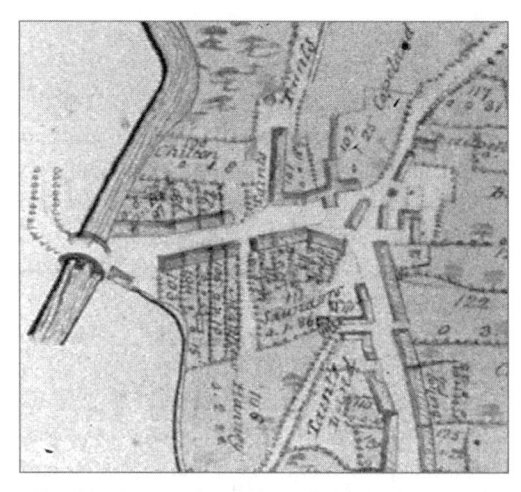

The 1806 map shows how Pensford's centre and market place appears to have been laid out, perhaps in the 14th century, to divert earlier north-south trackways

This may be thought unremarkable, and that any element of planning in the medieval era would be unlikely. However, features of planned village lay-outs from the medieval era are now widely recognised. For instance, it has been noted the basic plan of Hinton Blewett and East Harptree are very similar. [39]

Just as the construction of the A37 road in the early 19th century bypassed the High Street, the medieval line of the High Street bypassed the earlier 'Old Way'. See T45a (page 39) for a suggestion as to the route it might have taken.

The extent of the minor trackways which existed at different times all over the parish would be revealed more fully in a parish survey. The height of the banks and the depth of the track surface are obviously partly related to the nature of the soil or rock, and the gradient, but 'hollow ways' are usually ancient. The best example of a hollow way which is now derelict is the one in T305, but other tracks can be made out in T201, 105, 14, 58 and possibly 15. The T58 track looks from aerial photographs to have been a continuation of a track going from T45a towards Stanton Wick. Day and Masters' map of 1782 does indicate the existence of such a route, though not very precisely. [40]

As noted earlier, the ford indicated in the 12th century name 'Pendelsford' could have been Saxon or earlier, and could have related to the 'Old Way', see page 35. [41] The bridge which superseded the ford needed regular rebuilding and maintainance, judging by the earliest surviving records. In 1632 the bridges of Pensford and 'Woollworth' were in need of repair, [42] and again in 1652 after the 'greater part' of Pensford bridge had been beaten down by floods. [43] In 1653

Pensford Bridge was repaired for £35 [44] and in 1666 Pensford and Woollard bridges were again repaired, for £15.18. [45]

In 1727 Bristol Turnpike Trust was established to raise tolls on major roads out of Bristol, thereby to improve their condition. The roads continued to pose other hazards for travellers though: for example, in 1731 a traveller was 'very much wounded, assaulted and abused' by six men 'lifting up their cudgells in a very riotous and menacing manner' on the King's highway between Pensford and Clutton. [46]

In 1819 an Act for repairing, widening and improving several roads round Bristol was passed, and this specifies all the properties in Publow, together with the names of owner and tenant, through which the new road would go. The line of the main road built soon after 1819 is absent from the 1776 map, but visible on the 1839 map. On the later map it can be seen running on its present route from T22 to T142 (part is not shown shown, being in the parish of Stanton Drew). Note the modern bridge which carries the A37 over the River Chew, is a replacement for the bridge was destroyed in the floods of 1968. The single-arched stone bridge which it replaced is not shown on the 1839 map as it was built some time between 1839 and 1885 - see T22. Eleven properties in the 'parish of Pensford' were also specified in the 1819 Act.[47]

Various other reroutings of the A37 took place. The A37's line on Hursley Hill is at least the fourth route there (see T361, 363 and 365). Also, to the south of the parish the major route may once have been through T153, see below. At any rate, the Turnpike took considerable revenues. The Turnpike at Chelwood Gate (T152) took £475.0.0 in the year ending March 25th 1831 (Whitchurch Gate took £680 and Knowle Gate took £755). [48] The Popham accounts for 1826 note that 'By Chelwood Gate twice with a waggon' cost 2/6d.22. [49] The volume of paying carts per day therefore probably wasn't more than about 20. In 1867 Bristol Turnpike Trust was wound up - see T365.

Commons and Coalmines

Perhaps the most striking feature of the 1776 map of Publow is the extent of common land (see T58, 130, 197, 198, 199, 274, 299 etc) and patches of wood and possibly wood pasture (see T111 etc). If these areas could be shown not to have reverted to that state from previous cultivation, they would provide evidence of the lack of intensive use in the Anglo Saxon and early medieval era. This could have reflected the area's status as part of a minor estate (Belluton) or a minor, peripheral part of a major estate (Keynsham). In either case the underlying reason, literally enough, might be the soil - generally acidic where it is derived from the coal measures sandstones of most of the parish.

Most of these commons and woods were south of the Chew, and would represent the northern fringe of the Somerset territory noted earlier (page18) as corresponding to that of the last Celtic strongholds.

In 1776 of the 1,217 acres in the survey, 225 acres were listed as common land, mostly in four main blocks: Priest Down (T247, 14 acres, plus maybe more around T299), Birchwood and Lords Wood (T130 etc) together with Publow Common (T197 etc) (jointly totalled at 130 acres) Sideham Common (T58, 39 acres), Common Mead (T97, 10 acres). A further 80 acres were Glebe land (see T7-10) or Church land (see T136 etc), and another 40 acres were regarded as wastes or streets. By 1839 none of this was listed as common land, although probably various wide road verges would have been treated as common land - many of these surviving today. Sadly, several more have been appropriated by acquisitive adjacent landowners within the last two decades.

Coal mining in the parish has a long history, with various documentary records from the 17th century onwards, often associated with the commons mentioned above, see T58, T130, T157, T158, T166, T197, T299, T300, T304 etc. Several of those early records relate to the hazards created by early mines, and the remnants of some old bell pits are still visible, for example in T168. Other old bell pits show up as blackish circles in various fields around the parish after they have just been ploughed (eg T110).

Local mining developed with the technologies to allow deeper and deeper working, and bigger and bigger mines and collieries. For a summary of royalties from some of the coal mines on the Pophams' estate during the late 17th and early 18th century, see T166. These bell-pit mines would have preceded the longwall technique of mining which began to be used in Somerset from about 1725.

By the end of the 18th century Billingsley recorded that the depth of North Somerset pits varied from 60 to 80 fathoms (360 foot to 480 foot) and as early as 1610 a depth of 48 foot was recorded in a pit at Clutton. The Pophams had been content to take their freeshare rather than become involved as owners or shareholders in mining operations. [50] This was probably in the belief that the profits of mining were not equal to the risks - a view expressed by Billingsley. The Pophams did eventually take over full ownership of their mines from 1819-29, but by then most of the pits had been exhausted.[51]

The above-ground operations of the big coal mine known as Pensford Colliery from about 1910 to 1959 were in the parish of Stanton Drew, and so are-excluded form this study. However, (by way of excusing the inclusion here of the 1910 photograph) the underground workings of Pensford Colliery extended far and wide below ground - the only 'out of bounds' area was that below the big railway viaduct built in the 1870s.

At a test borehole in field T360, in the north of the parish, Pensford No 1 seam was struck at 1,724 foot, No 2 at 1,884 foot, and No 3 at 1,889 foot below sea level (add 221 foot for the depth below surface).[A12] Coal-mining was probably a source of employment for local people continuously from the 16th to the 20th centuries. All of the available local Census data, from 1841 to 1901, shows shows numbers of coal miners employed locally.

In the 1901 Census, before Pensford Colliery opened, 22 men and one woman are listed as having occupations directly connected with coalmining, probably in largeish collieries - a number of local parishes had working mines within walking distance. Whether the individual's work was above or below ground is generally noted, and four men are listed as 'banksman'. Banksmen were probably responsible for controlling mine shaft top and signalling cages for men and coal, etc. The ages of the colliery workers were from 14 to 80 - and the 80 year-old's 76 year-old wife was listed as a coal haulier! A list of the names and ages of the 23 people is on the website: www.biografix.co.uk

Miscellaneous

Chapels and Churches. See T1, T17, T231, T316, T317, T340
Chapels, non-conformist. See T162, T17, T131.
Crime and punishment. See T91
Lime kilns. See T164, T165, T168, T385, T393, T394.
Markets & fairs. See T45 and T91
Mills. See T85, T154, T183, T186, T187, T191, T209, T253.
Tanneries. See T207, T232, T268, T272.

GAZETTEER

The following sequence of numbers is taken from the 1839 Publow Parish Tithe Map, which is shown in this book on pages 86 to 91. The description after the T number is from the Tithe apportionment, and the numbers and letters in brackets after this give the respective map page references.

Publow Church, 1916

T1 Publow Churchyard (88 B2). The Perpendicular Church tower was regarded by Pevsner, and others, as appearing to beC14 rather than C15. The church at Publow was probably founded from Keynsham, as were those of Queen Charlton, Whitchurch, Chewton Keynsham and Brislington. They continued to pay annual homage and dues to Keynsham throughout the Middle Ages and later. See the introductory section on 'Settlements' for more on the probable role of Keynsham Abbey in establishing Pensford as a market town.

T2 House and garden Belleview (88 B2). This is shown in William Curtis's painting of Publow Church, c1840, as having a tiled roof, [52] but in the Hunstrete Estate Sale Catalogue of 1911 it is described as two stone built thatched cottages.

T3 The pound (88 B2. This had also gone by 1885, to be replaced by the pound still visible an the NE corner of T4. See also T116.

T3a House, garden and orchard (88 B2). In 1873 this was described as a 'ruinous cottage', [53] and by 1885 it had been demolished.

T5 Butts Mead (88 B2). This name could be derived from archery butts, a facility the manor had to provide in medieval times for training the nation's archers. The topography would be suitable: a level field with a steep natural bank at one end. In 1776 the field was called 'The mead', with an annotation 'called Biss Mead', probably after the clothier John Bisse, who probably owned most of Belluton and Pensford by 1562.

T7-10 Parsonage Farm and attached Glebe land (88 B1). The Glebe Lands of the parish were let to various tenants in order to provide a living for the rector, and for nearly all parishes they were subject to the jurisdiction of the local diocese. However, in 1846, the Reverend James Daubeny somehow managed to successfully sell off all the Publow Glebe lands. The Reverend Andrew Daubeny had been rector from 1797, when the rectory was settled on him by his father another Andrew Daubeny.

A document of 1600 records that T7-10 had been granted to Henry VIII's sixth and surviving wife Katherine Parr (not Ann Boleyn, as local legend claims), who had also been given Queen Charlton in 1544. [5] Katherine died in 1548 and her second husband, Thomas Lord Seymour, was executed the following year for high treason. Publow's Glebe Lands as recorded in 1839 were probably much the same as they would have been when they were allocated, probably in the late medieval era. The full list of Glebe lands in 1839: T1, 7, 8, 9, 10, 241, 249, 289, 307, 308a, 311, 312, 324, 331, 333, 349, 357, 376, 379, 387, 393. See also 309, 330 etc.

T11 Butts Markham. (88 A1) In 1776 this was just 'Butts'. Unlike T5, above, the derivation in this case is probably 'butte', a section of the common arable field shorter than the rest. These strips are more easily seen on the 1776 map, but the major part of the arable field was to the west in Belluton. In 1776 the name 'Markham' was only applied to T14, see below.

T12 Butts. (88 A1) As above

T13 Paddock. (88 A1) Shown as 'Butts' in 1776.

T14 Stratton Hill. (88 A2)The name Stratton was taken from the tenant of 1776, at which time T14 was called 'a close called Markham'. Leases of 1738, 1758 and 1763 give the form Marcombe, [54] Although the 'comb' suffix is the earlier recorded name, the 'ham' seems more likely as the original meaning, from the Old English 'ham', especially applied to riverside meadows. More interesting is the prefix, possibly derived from the OE 'mearc' - land on a boundary. Perhaps this relates to a boundary of the Belluton estate in Saxon times (see the introductory section on boundaries).

The leases refer to Marcombe as 'lately held by Edward Lock, deceased, and now by Peter Lock'. Edward Lock was in 1656 the petty constable of Pensford (see T86). John Locke (1632-1704), the famous philosopher, inherited property in Belluton after his father's death in 1661. Accounts of the Puritan Somerset household in which Locke grew up provide an interesting perspective on the 'riotous behaviour' in Pensford reported by Edward Lock in 1656 (see T86). John Locke never married, left no heirs, and spent much of his time abroad after accusations in 1678 that he was involved in conspiring on behalf of Monmouth. But, as various publications on the life and letters of Locke show, he retained numerous friends and contacts in Somerset. See page 7.

T15 Long Barhams. (88 B2) Another riverside 'ham', the hedge dividing it from

T16 looks relatively recent, ie probably 18th or 17th century. All the -hams in the flood plane of the River Chew would have a long history of being valued grazing or meadow land on account of their fertility being regularly replenished by floods. The 'Bar-' prefix is sometimes derived from 'bere', hard barley, and this might have been grown on the upper level of T15 and 16. Or OE 'baere': woodland + acorns. [105]

T16 Barhams. (88 B2) The upper level was acquired as the village's sports field around 1949, after Pensford Football Club had been told it could no longer use T98. It had been used before this for cricket matches.

T17 Orchard. (88 A1) In 'Small Medieval Towns in Avon', Roger Leech refers to this as 'Chapel Barton', suggesting that the name was derived from the former site of a chapel demolished in the mid-17th century, but it's unlikely that 'Chapel Barton' was correctly applied to T17. It could have been taken from a map where it was intended to apply to T20 (see below). Equally, although it's thought that a chapel existed somewhere called 'Borough Bank' in Publow and was demolished in the mid-17th century, this may well not be the site - perhaps it was at T316. This Orchard was attached to the King's Arms, see below. The field name 'Capell' by the side of the road at Publow Hill also suggests a site that deserves some archaeological investigation - see T316. There is also a 'Chapel Piece' by Birchwood Lane (see T131), and a former Presbyterian meeting house now called 'Chapel Cottage', at Whitley Batts - see T162.

T18 The Kings Arms. (88 A2) The first record of this pub so far noted is 1757 when Henry Sage acquired it from Susanna Corp. It was still shown as The Kings Arms in 1839. Both maps suggest that another frontage of the pub was east-facing, in which case the space in front of it could have formed an important extension to the market area. Noted as Copeland in 1806. See also T313, Sage's Vineyards.

T19 House and garden. (88 A2) Described as a house and wheelwright's shop in 1806.

T20 Cottages and Gardens. (88 A2) 'Chapel Barton' (see T17), this is listed in the 1901 Census as a small street containing nine small cottages, eight of which only had two or one occupants, most of them elderly. This is roughly where the Wesleyan Chapel was, the chapel being converted to 3 houses around 1885. The 1776 map shows a small building by the road which was tenanted by 'The Parish'. A map of 1806 suggests a plan of what could be an octagonal shaped building. Somerset Record Office has registers of this Wesleyan Chapel chapel from 1794 to 1837. In 1739 Wesley recorded that he preached every other Thursday 'near Pensford', probably again at Priest Down, though he also preached in at least one house in Pensford, in 1760. See T250 and T274.

T22 Garden. (88 A2) Just a garden in 1839, but soon to be bisected by the extension of the turnpike road to the site of the new bridge. There is said to have been a hat factory here later in the 19th century. In 1776 there were five cottages, possibly preserving the plots of medieval tenements, and possibly looking much like those in the old photo of thatched cottages in T23-25 (see the back cover).

T23 House and shop. (88 A2) In 1806 a smith's shop. This is the end house as shown in the photograph on the back cover. It looks like it could be a 16th century building, but a document in Somerset Record Office's Popham archive contains a 1737 reference to shops 'recently built' and standing near the bridge at Pensford. [56] In 1839 this building was owned by Popham, and occupied by James Higgins, who also had the garden at T26.

T24 Cottage and Garden. (88 A2) 1839 occupier: William Hathway.

T25 House and garden. (88 A2) 1839 occupier: Hannah Lowe.

T26 Garden. (88 A2) now the garden of Coombe House.

T29 House and yard. (88 A2) Now called Shumach House. In 1806 this was noted as 'a good house and butcher's shop', with a 'pleck of land' over the road, the near half of T94. The lessee was Martha Green, widow of Richard Green. Martha Green had in 1794 gone into partnership with John Green in a butchers and farmers business. [57] Perhaps they were related to the Green of Green's Folly, see T85. Another Green was a butcher at Compton Dando: in 1797 James Green was bound over in the sum of £50 not to cut down or damage any of Pophams' trees, and was also told to sow with grass a close he had cleared and ploughed. [58]

T30 House, yards and orchard. (88 A2) The 1776 map and survey appears to show this as 'butcher's market'.

T32 Cottage and garden. (88 A2) This building had been demolished by 1885. An opportunity to check the origins of the building arose in 1986 with the construction of a new house on the site, but this was not taken. As Roger Leech said in 'Small Medieval Towns in Avon' (1975): 'Pensford's early history can only be unravelled by archaeological research ... all sites within areas of archaeological interest will need to be watched (often by local groups) in the course of contractors' works'. There have been a few opportunities for archaeological research in Pensford with developments, such as excavations for the sewage works and system installed around 1994. Nothing very significant has been recorded, but the archaeological monitoring was fairly minimal.

T33 Cottages and Gardens. (88 A2) The Old Bakery. In 1776 this is number 51 on the rent roll and was tenanted by 'The Club'. One other reference to a club has been discovered, a synonym for the Brotherly Society instituted in 1769, and of which Joseph Heath (a cordwainer or shoemaker) was the steward in 1783. [110] The map, and the plural 'Cottages', seem to indicate a building on the corner of the High Street and the lane running down to Salters Brook. It seems to have been knocked down some time after 1839. The other 'Cottage' was probably The Old Bakery, in which the old bread oven is still preserved, though possibly this could have been property 52 on the 1776 survey, and no information is provided for that number. In 1839 the property 'Cottages and Gardens' was owned and occupied by William Flower. In 1901 it was noted as 'Baker's Shop', occupied by George Smart (38), his wife Annie (40), their daughter Doris, and Henry Primrose (21) 'journeyman baker'. Primrose and his local bakery deliveries are still remembered by older Pensford residents.

T35 House, shop and yard. (88 A2)

T36 Cottages and gardens. (88 A2) In 1806 this appears to have been two tenements and a wheelwright's shop.

T40 Strip. (88 A3) The remnant of T39, left when the turnpike road was driven through, in 1806. Halfpenny well can still be seen by the path above Salter's Brook here.

T43 Orchard. (88 A3) An Iron Age coin, an uninscribed gold stater was found here by Mr C.Hudson while digging the foundations of a bungalow. One side of the coin showed a stylised head, the other a triple tailed horse with a crab shaped device beneath. [59] The coin was bought by Bristol City Museum, and Mr Hudson should be thanked for making it available - unlike those who do not allow their 'finds' to be properly identified and recorded.

T45a Pensford Down. (88 A3) Shown in 1776 as part of 'The Common, Down, etc'. As an element in settlement names '-dun' is used for a low hill 'with a fairly level and fairly extensive summit which provided a good settlement-site in open country' (Gelling and Cole). There are alternative possibilities of OE or OW derivations, according to the situation. A suggestion that Pensford Down is an older settlement nucleus, on an older route than the High St, is provided by an item in the Popham Court Papers for 15.5.1763: 'We do present and order the Old Way from Pensford Down to the Middle Gate or place where a gate formerly stood to a ground called the conygre belonging to Mr Adams to be made by midsummer next by such person or persons who have diverted it'. This 'Old Way' could well start with the lanes which still more or less exist on a direct line from the medieval Pensford bridge up to the council estate now on T45a - but in medieval times and possibly earlier, T45a was a village green.

The route south from here would have been the part obstructed in 1763. The 'conygre' mentioned is not likely to be T125, 131, 132 or 210 (see below) but is probably one off the Publow map, west of T140, in Stanton Drew parish, which has a history of landhold-

T45a is the plot at the bottom of this photo, with the first council houses in it (aerial photo from 1946)

ing by the Adams family. This 'Middle Gate' could be indicated as a small nick in the outline of the parish boundary, as shown on the 1776 map. It could also be close to one of the possible sites of the 'antient pound' referred to in the 1671 account of the boundaries of Publow parish (see the introductory section on Estate and Parish Boundaries, and notes on T116). This Old Way probably ran through the green at T45a to pass between T62 and 116 and on the join Old Road above its current junction with the A37. It was presumably already relatively disused in 1763 for someone to have imagined they would get away with diverting it. T45a was probably also the site of the old sheep fairs, see T91, and similar events.

T57 Cottage and paddock. (88 A3) This plot of just over an acre was described as 'arable' in 1839. The cottage had been demolished by the time of the 1885 map.

T58 Sideham. (88 A3) Probably part of a bigger common once shared with Stanton Drew, see page 28, 'Commons'. The name isn't given in the 1776 records, and the first form of the name so far noted is Sidon. From the court papers for 23.10.1789: 'we present an old coal pit on Sidon to be open and very dangerous and that the Lady of the manor [Dorothy Popham] fills up the same'. In 1791 it is referred to as Sidonham. Side-down makes most sense as the derivation, going by topography and land-use. The surviving remnant of old pasture, now part of Nursery Farm, is botanically very rich and may never have been ploughed. Broad-leaved Ragwort (Senecio fluviatilis) grows by the brook. J.W.White wrote (in 'The Bristol Flora', 1912) that the first British record was 1680, between Glastonbury and Wells. However, Nicholas Culpepper had already noted in 1653 that it grew in waters and woodsides, and that the Germans valued its medicinal qualities above all other herbs 'of the same quality'. [60] So, it could be a relic of cultivation, as at T102 and a few other spots by the Chew.

T59 Cottage and garden. (88 A3) This building is shown as surviving to 1885, but by then the present Nursery Farm had also been built. By the edge of T57, there is an oak tree which was measured as having a 22ft 6in circumference (at 5ft off the ground) in 1985, making it the third biggest oak recorded in the Chew Valley at that time.

T63 Cottages and gardens. (88 A3) A Roman coin here was dug up by Mr F.Baum and presented to Taunton Museum in 1931. The date is 305-313AD, Maximus II.

T80 School House and garden. (88 A3) The Education Returns to Parliament of 1833 listed five daily schools and two Sunday schools.

T81 House and garden. (88 A2) In 1806 listed as 'house in 2 tenements and shoemaker's shop'.

T82 House and garden. (88 A2) In 1806 listed as 'house and baker's shop'.

T84 House and Paddock. (88 A2) This is the house next to Green's Folly, now known as Viaduct View. When Somerset and South Avon Vernacular Building Research Group members visited selected Pensford buildings, at my invitation, on March 12 1988, the major revelation of the day was that this building contained an early 16th century cruck construction. Crucks are basically two very large upright beams making a sort of 'A' shape, or series of 'A' shapes, around which a house was built. There are very few other known examples of crucks surviving in this part of Somerset, and

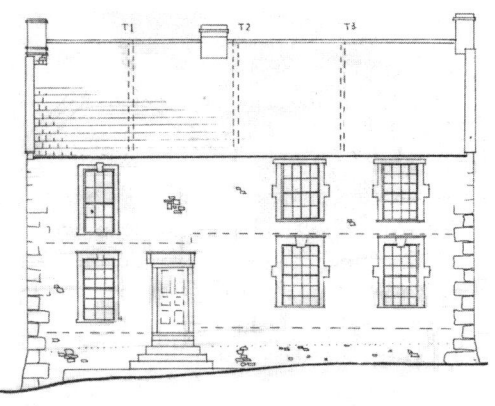

Elevation of Viaduct View, the hatched lines in the roof showing the position of the crucks

this discovery, by John Dallimore, was fairly unexpected. This, and the fine Tudor fireplace within the house, provide a unique relic of the prosperity of medieval Pensford. A dendrochronological investigation into the age of the oak timber in the house subsequently established a felling date of 1512 for the timber. [61] Bridge House, by the medieval Pensford bridge, and just outside the old parish of Publow, is one of the few other local buildings to retain features from that era. In 1839 T84 was owned by Popham, and tenanted by Ezekiel Harris. In 1901 it appears to have been a bakery, occupied by Henry (49) and Ann (50) Blanning and their four children, three of whom are listed as 'assistant baker'. This is despite the existence of the baker's shop opposite at T33, with its own bread oven. From about 1979 to 1981 Robert Hunter lived here with Maureen Leppard, before they moved to Marin County, California and married. Although successfully preserving his anonymity here at the time, as lyricist for the Hunter-Garcia songwriting partnership with Gerry Garcia, he wrote the words for most of the songs on the albums of the Grateful Dead. They were, and still are (despite Garcia's death in 1993), one of the most commercially successful and musically respected bands of the late 20th century.

T85 Cottages and Gardens. (88 A2) Green's Folly. In 1806 listed as 'range of buildings in 5 tenements, lessee Mrs Green', hence the name applied to it then and now, 'Green's Folly'. This Mrs Green was the widow of Daniel Green, which can be seen from the 1806 listing for Paradise Row, Woollard, of which she was also lessee. Most of the range is not listed in the 1776 survey, implying that it was not owned by the Pophams, but the end of the terrace was listed, and the map shows a distinctive short tenement similar to the possibly medieval ones in T22 and higher up the High St. These are best seen in the 1806 copy of the 1776 map. The building was presumably rebuilt in 1782, as indicated by the present date-stone. The instigator of this, and the 1782 reconstruction of Paradise Row, was probably Daniel Green. No evidence for a connection has yet been found, but he way well have been a senior figure in the briefly prosperous copper company Tyndall and Elton, [62] and the cottages could have been renovated to provide accommodation for skilled workers. 'Tyndall Esq & Co' were listed as tenants of Woollard Great Mill and New Mill (the wire mill) in 1776 - see below, T229 and 187. T85 and part of Paradise Row were both owned, not by the Pophams, but by Mary Ward, in 1839. The Hunstrete Estate accounts for 1822 list George Ward as tenant of a mill and 33 acres, [63] while a Richard Brickdale Ward is named in a court case of 1851 involving the John Freeman & Copper Company, [64] which may have taken over Tyndall and Elton in the 1790's.

T86 George Inn and Garden. (88 A2) In 1806 this was indicated as an Inn with associated stables, house, bakehouse, garden and orchard, though it's not possible to tell from the map which was which building. The lane leading up between T86 and T88 is probably where the double gates next to No 148 High St are now. The 1776 map shows this lane to be lined with buildings either side, and a lot of these could have been stables, and most of them had gone by 1839. Perhaps this was the main site for the stabling for 102 horses said to be available in Pensford in 1686, in a survey made for the military. 20 guest beds were also available then, although, as with the stabling, the Kings Arms (T17) might also have figured in these totals. The earliest reference to The George so far found: information given to Richard Jones on the 29th April 1656 by Edward Lock, petty constable of Pensford (see T14, probably the uncle of John Locke, the philosopher) concerning 'riotous behaviour of certain persons the day after the fair at Pensford at the George Inn and afterwards in the street, whereby the said constable and his assistants were much ill-treated.' [65]

T90 Two cottages. (88 A2) The ruins of one of these is shown in the painting of the lock up c1890, by E.Parkman, shown on the opposite page. [66]

T91 Two cottages. (88 A2) These were demolished by the time of this painting. Opposite this, where the triangular green now is, there was the market hall, demolished some time between 1806 and 1839. This was probably a late medieval building, and the fragments of sculpture now preserved in the cottages at the back of the Miners Hall may have come from a medieval market cross somewhere close to the market hall, (see page 24) although there's no evidence to prove it. Pensford Market figures several times in the Hunstrete Estate accounts for 1705 and 1713. [67] In 1705 Lambrook Long paid £6 for the rental on Pensford markets and fairs, but was paid 1/6d for hurdles for Pensford market - the area where animals could have been penned may have been T30 or T18. Hurdles would have been used at the two fairs per year up at T45a, but this reference is clearly 'for Pensford market'. In 1713 Lambrook Long was paid 2/4d for repairing the standings. In a fascinating account of some Pensford recollections written by Holly Batten shortly before he died in 1987, he referred to the use of these surviving into the late 19th century: 'The big day in Pensford in my

The lock-up c1890, by E.Parkman.

parents' day was Whit Wednesday, this is when the Clubs would walk to Church. It was a holiday, and up the High Street there would come the standings - these were stalls similar to the ones you see in the markets of today.' [68] He also referred to an old sheep fair on the site of the former council houses at T45a, and a hurdle house similar to that still existing at the village green at Priddy (which still holds its annual sheep fair on the third Wednesday of August). According to the Kelly's Directory of 1914, Pensford's fairs were formerly held on the 6th of May and the 8th of November in each year 'but are now extinct.' In 1791 Collinson noted that Pensford was a small 'but ancient' market town, and that its market day was Tuesday. Market matters figure frequently in the court papers, for instance in 1756: 'All persons who allow their courts, yards or bartons in the Town of Pensford to be used on market days for exposing any pigs for sale are to be fined 6/8d in each case. No dung or rubbish to be dumped where the pig market is now kept'. Or from 1673: 'Wee presente all ye inhabytence of Pensford that they keep in their swine markett days and that they Rid and carry away all such swile as lyeth in ye streete upon ye paine of 3/4d each person making defaulte'.

The market was also considered the best time and place for public punishment, and this explains the site of the lock-up, and maybe the village stocks which preceded it on that spot. The lock-up itself, thought to date from about 1750, naturally doesn't appear in the Tithe schedule, as a (normally) non-residential building.

In the early 17th century, alleged offenders were brought in from various neighbouring villages to be publicly whipped in Pensford's market place, on market day. Incidentally, Maurice Cranston quotes from John Locke Senior's journal to to attach some blame to him personally for this vicious expression of the prevalent puritanism. [10] An entry in Locke's journal headed 'Bastardie' specifies that an unmarried mother be taken to a public place 'stripped from the middle upward' and whipped 'until her body be bloodie - twice'. [69] However, Locke was probably just noting instructions received from the Justices of the Peace for the local division - Francis Baber and Sir Thomas Bridges - years earlier. These two signed orders using the exact wording quoted by Locke above in his journal, against other unmarried mothers, in 1614, 1616 and 1617. [70] The 'twice' meant that the victim had to suffer the same treatment in Pensford's market place, and then again in their home village (Cameley, Burnet and Compton Dando, respectively). Locke Senior, born in 1606, might even have witnessed these events as a youngster, but in any event, they were not his invention. He is reputed to have worked later as a clerk for Francis Baber (1565-1643), of Chew Magna, youngest son of Edward Baber (1531-1578), whose memorial effigy is in Chew Magna Church). Sir Thomas Bridges (1567-1621) was the grandson of the Sir Thomas Bridges who bought Keynsham Abbey and its lands in 1552 (the manor of Keynsham remained with the Crown from 1539 until it was sold in 1613).

T92 Cottages and yards. (88 A2) The cottage next to the lock-up is pictured in the c1890 painting. The one further north was destroyed by fire in 1885, according to a note in a Popham Estate rent roll of about 1906. [A9]

T94 Garden. (88 A2) see T29. Publow allotments had been laid out over this plot on their present plan by 1871, by the Popham estate. The estate sold the allotments to Somerset County Council for £110 in 1917, and Publow Parish Council bought them from SCC for £162.12.0 in 1920, the mortgage being redeemed in 1951. [71]

T96 Publow Hill. (88 B2) In 1776 referred to as 'The Hill or Wood' and 1806 shown as Publow Wood. The 1776 map shows a belt of trees extending as far as the road, and also a building at its eastern edge, at the bottom of a trackway which probably pre-dates the field pattern shown (the trackway is still visible). A fine old oak tree here, visible on the horizon when viewed from the road below, was measured in 1985 as having an 18ft circumference, making it the eleventh biggest recorded in the Chew Valley.

T97 Common Mead. (88 B2) This odd shaped plot of land is not shown in 1776, but by 1806 had been staked out as a strip on the western edge of 'Common Meadow'. This looks like a dole, a strip allocation with-in a communal hay meadow, but despite the name, the 1776 map seems to contradict this. By 1873 it had been acquired by the Rev A.Bellamy, and in that year was incorporated into the Popham Estate after an exchange deal which gave the vicar the site of the parsonage he then built on T211 and 212. [53]

T98 Common Mead. (88 B2) In 1776 this had 6 major divisions, which the 1806 map shows were hedged. The hedge along the southern boundary could have been an ancient one, separating the wood pasture to the south from the meadow to the north, but by 1885 it had been grubbed up. However its line is still very visible, particularly where it curves in to the road. The 1776 map shows 'Mr

Owen's Duckpools', and pool-shapes are still visible after flooding or heavy rain. Could they have originated as fish ponds in the Keynsham Abbey era? Medieval fishpond relics, which may or may not be comparable, exist at Cameley. The triangular plot in which the 'Mr' is written on the 1776 map was in 1806 a withy bed. Yet another land use devised by a later generation was football (see T16). The north west quarter of the field in 1776 was referred to as Ducknest.

T102 Henpound. (88 B2) No clues as to whether this refers to hens or game birds, or actual impoundment of stray hens. In 1776 this was called Kinsham. Another riverside -ham, but the 1806 map shows it as Keynsham's Meadow, and this is probably the original form, from medieval ownership by Keynsham Abbey. Note, immediately to the south are the possible fishponds (T98) and immediately to the north is a possible medieval rabbit warren (see below, T210). There are still a few unusual plants here which could also be relics of monastic cultivation. In 'The Bristol Flora' (1912) one of to the contributors to J.W.White's book is quoted as noting soapwort (Saponaria officinalis): 'in plenty at Publow on the left bank of the Chew, in a meadow below the bridge; all the plants with double flowers.' I found one such plant here in 1986. Broad-leaved Ragwort (Senecio fluviatilis) also still grows here, and could have been originally introduced for its reputed medicinal properties see T58.

T103 Alderwells. (88 B2) Called Alderwell in 1776. Wells meant springs, which can still be seen here, as can alders.

T104 Long Alderwells. (92 B2) As above.

T105 Publow Wood. (88 B2) Just 'The Wood' in 1776.

T106 Tyning. (88 B2) Called 'The Tining' in 1776. Other tynings occur at T350, 371,373, 375, and 403, and all appear to be associated with late medieval arable cultivation. Tyning generally means a (fenced) enclosure, and the word was originally Old English. The 1806 map shows T106 as arable with furrows running west to east, but in 1839 it was down to pasture. By 1885 T106 had been incorporated into one huge field by grubbing up hedges between it and T107, 87, 108, 109 and 110. However, some of the best trees in the old hedges were left and are shown on the 1885 map. Some of these survived for another 70 years or so and are shown on an aerial photo of 1958. [72] In 1987 this large field was ploughed again after many years under pasture, and farmer Colin Smart gave permission for the Publow Survey team, organised by Barbara Bowes, to 'field walk' it. A large quantity of medieval and post-medieval pottery fragments was found, and the more interesting of these were displayed in the Becket Centre, having been identified by Bristol City Museum. Most dates from the 17th and 18th centuries, and would have probably have been spread on the land with household refuse thrown in the privy.

T107 Corn Close. (88 B2) Probably a similar history to 106. A two acre Corn Close mentioned in a 1758 lease may be the same field. The line of the hedge between

Trees surviving until 1885 (map) and 1946 (photo) from old hedges around T108 it and T87, grubbed up over a hundred years ago, can still be seen after ploughing.

T108 'Oatley Close and Calves Close' (88 B3) is the title on the Tithe apportionment. The 1776 survey shows the western half of T108 as Catley. There are several examples of names being altered by apparent misreading rather than mishearing (see also T115 and 390). The 1839 names my seem more logical, but this may be the result of imposition of logic by the Tithe map surveyor. John Field commented that genuinely old field names prefixed 'cat' do actually refer to wild cats. Until relatively recently, the 1940s, the field was a popular play space with Pensford village children, and was referred to as K's. The 1776 map provides the derivation of this: James Cave's five closes. No Caves appear on the 1806 survey, so the name K's suggests some 150 years of oral tradition and modification.

T109 Alderwell. (88 B3) See T103

T110 Sandhills. (88 B3) Shown as Sandhole in 1776, which way perhaps have been derived from a pit where some of the sandy soil might have been extracted. Ploughing in 1987 also revealed a black shaley circle of some 20 yards diameter near the junction with T109, presumably the remnant of a coal pit - see below T168. The 1:10,560 geological survey of the area shows this field to be around the northern tip of an area of red calcareous sandstone extending down to about T160 [A13]. This may have been recognised in or before the Anglo Saxon era as both fertile and easily worked, hence 'The Lye' - see introduction and below T122.

T111 Grove Piece. (88 B3) In 1776 this was 3 plots, Grove was the largest, to the east, a middle block called 'adjoining Groves' and to the west an acre of woodland. The 1776 map shows a large number of trees and this would appear to be the mid-point of a belt of woodland which my have stretched from Lord's Wood (T173) westward to T96, avoiding the area of better soil referred to above. This belt is shown on the geological map as 'undivided, mainly mudstone' with occasional sandstone bands and fragments. 'Grove' is from the OE 'graf', a copse or small wood, implying that this had been separated from any continuous belt of woodland at the time the name was first applied. Other 'Grove' names are at T127, 129, 131, 215, 218, and 303. Looking at a possible distinction between these and areas shown as or called 'wood', the groves may have been wood-pasture, with some grass and animals allowed to graze, much as T105 is now, whereas animals might have been excluded from 'wood' to prevent them from eating coppice regrowth.

T114 Crabtree Close. (88 B3) Just called 'A Close' on the 1776 survey, so the name 'crabtree' probably comes from a distinctive old crab apple tree in the field in the early 19th century. The apples on a genuine wild crab apple (Malus sylvestris) are about an inch in diameter, and examples can still be found locally.

T115 Moorcroft. (88 B3) See below, T140. Called 'Great Lyfield' on the 1776 survey, see T122.

T116 Pound Close and Hollybushes. (88 A3) The 1776 map shows an odd mixture of a central plot called 'Hollybushes', containing trees, quite possibly similarly in character to the rough grazing of the adjoining common, and various strips which were probably cultivated as arable. They probably represent the last phase of privatisation of formerly common land. The 1806 map shows that the two strips to the north (marked 'Stocker' and 'A.Adams') had by then been combined and shown as Pound Close. This is the only evidence available for trying to say where the 'antient pound' was ('ye lord's pound' - see the 1671 account quoted in the the introductory section on Estate and Parish Boundaries, and notes on T45a). This suggests the pound could have been up in the northern corner somewhere, next to the road, and it would have been used to impound stray or unauthorised animals from commons to the west and east. However, the southern edge of T116, where it joins the boundary of Stanton Drew, and where intercommoning was probably taking place, makes a more logical situation for a pound, and one more likely to have been included as a boundary marker in the the 1671 account. That could raise questions as to the earlier status of the track leading around the western edge of T116, and then through T45a up into Pensford.

T117 Blues. (88 A3) Simply 'a close by Hollybushes' in 1776, and 'top ground' in 1806. Blues might have been referring to wild flowers such as scabious or meadow cranesbill. This isn't very convincing, but at any rate 'blues' may relate to a feature of pasture rather than ploughed ground, as it was pasture in 1839.

T118 Home Meads.(88 B3) 'Home' is usually applied to the field or fields nearest the farmstead, in this case Leigh Farm. The line of the old hedge between T118 and 116 is still very visible. Possible earlier earthworks of indeterminate date and function have been noted from aerial photos. [73]

T119 Lower Orchard. (88 B3)

T120 House, yards and garden. (88 B3) Shown in 1776 as Homestead at the Lye.

T121 Orchard. (88 B3)

T122 Home orchard. (88 B3) In 1776 a homestead and an orchard both referred to as Hawting at the Lye after the tenant. Mr Hawting's holding consisted of these, the acre wood (see T111) and part of T113, which seems to have been extended westward slightly by 1839. The curved line of the north west edge of T122 may represent the line within which woodland was originally cleared in the Saxon era. However, these patterns were all destroyed between 1839 and 1885 with the shaping of the present Leigh Farm. Although T122 may have been one focus of settlement at The Lye, another existed at South Leigh Farm (T169),and it may not be possible to say which one was earlier or more significant. The perambulation of the Bounds of Publow of 1671 (see page 2) was probably referring to South Leigh Farm as 'ley', judging by the probable route.

T124 Shutty Mead. (88 B3) In 1776 this was two fields, the northern half being Shutty Mead, and the southern half called The Mead or Pool Mead. A remotely possible derivation of 'shutty': OE 'sciete' meaning 'corner or nook; outlying strip of land; piece of land projecting beyond another' - from 'English Field Names'.

T125 Conygre. (88 B3) Spelt Conygear in 1776. Coneygre means rabbit warren, and is usually taken to mean a place where a warren was established artificially in the medieval era (rabbits are not native animals, they were brought over by the Normans). Some of the sandier soils of the locality would have been suitable for this. However, the word 'coneygre' was also applied to areas where warrens were established naturally by the hardier rabbits of later centuries. The origins of each coneygre, and there are coneygres at T132 and T210 as well as the one west of T140 (see T45a) could only be established by further documentary or archaeological evidence. See below T210.

T126 Pool Mead. (88 B3) Shown as two fields in 1776, the southern being Pool Mead, and the northern being Lydown. The areas immediately north and east of this Lower Lydown were still common land in 1776, and the northern and eastern hedges of Lower Lydown probably represent early enclosures, perhaps 16th century, within the common . The western edge of Lower Lydown was an old trackway leading from The Lye to Publow (see also T201).

T127 Grove Mead. (88 B3) Called 'A Plow'd Orchard' in 1776. See T111

T128 Common. (88 B3) Part of Common by name in 1839, but no longer indicated as common land. In 1776 it was indicated as still part of the 130 acre expanse of common land. See T197 etc.

T129 Grove Meadow. (88 B3) In 1776 The Grove, a nine acre field of possible wood pasture, with the main concentration of trees in the south. Between 1806 and 1839 this had been altered to the shape shown on the Tithe map, and by 1885 it had been incorporated with T130 as one field, as it is now. See T111.

T130 Common. (88 B3) Altered successively, as T129. The trackway shown at the north edge of 130 is not shown on the 1776 map, but then common land was often traversed by many tracks. The simplest policy for the map maker would be not to show any of them. Probably the northern hedge of 130 was aligned along an existing trackway. The overall expanse of common land of which this was still part in 1776 seems to have been referred to by various names: Publow Common, Birchwood Common, Leigh Down Common, Lye Common, etc. In 1672 Sir Francis Popham signed a license for coal extraction from Burch Wood and Burchwood Common, and all other 'waste' in Publow. Such waste would be an obvious target for miners, and such coal mining probably already had a long history in Publow. The problem of old pits noted at T58 also occurred here, as the Publow court papers for May 8th 1721 show: Richard Brown was presented for 'Leaving open ye Colepitt Holls on Leigh Down Common and for carrying turfs and soyle from the common'. [28] As noted in the introductory section on 'Commons and Coalmines', a remarkably high proportion of the parish's area was still common land in 1776.

T131 Chapel Piece. (88 B3) The 1839 Chapel piece included part of the 1776 'The Grove', and the original Chapel Piece is shown on the 1776 map as the slightly diamond shaped field of 2 acres. Does this name imply Chapel ownership or use, or the actual site of a Chapel? Since the land use again looks unintensive, pasture with trees, perhaps this is the site of the 'lost' chapel referred to by Collinson (see T17,T231 and T316). If this were the case, it would not have been as remote as it now seems, as Birchwood Lane might have been well used as the route to Woollard, which also contained a medieval chapel at T231.

T132 Further Coneygre. (91 A2) Had the same name in 1776.

T133 Lye Down. (91 A2) In 1776 this was in two halves, the northern part called Upper Lydown, and the southern part called Home Ground. The area from here north to T126, Lower Lydown, presumably marks a previous edge of the common grazing suggested by 'down', and perhaps once covered by the sheep which contributed to Pensford's cloth trade in the 15th and 16th centuries. However, the Home Ground part of T133 might have been cultivated as arable in the medieval era. The strips of 136 and 137 were both marked out with stones, which generally indicates strips in an arable field. See below T136.

T134 Beadons. (91 A2) Shown as Beadams, araballly cultivated, in 1806, and as Bitham in 1776. The earlier form could be derived from OE 'bita' and 'ham', ie a small enclosure by a river. Although the adjacent brook has almost disappeared through abstraction at the source, it was formerly substantial and constant. John Field commented: 'Field names of the form 'Bittom', 'Bitham(s)', 'Beethem' etc are not unusual. Gloucestershire examples: Bittums (Horsely), Bitten Wall (Donnington), Bittum (Colesborne), Bittom (North Cerney). Apart from 'valley bottom', the term is used in some areas to mean water meadows.' This meadow is probably too steep to have been used as a water meadow, however. An alternative, possibly more interesting explanation is given in 'The Landscape of

Place-Names' (2000): 'beden or byden is sometimes used of deep valleys ... and when combined with terms for springs ... refers to a drinking vessel or to a container which holds water from the spring'. There was an excellent spring at the eastern end of T134, and the line of the ensuing brook can be seen in the line of field edges running all the way north to the Chew. See T203.

135 Burdens. (90 B2) Called The Paddock in 1806 and 1776, although probably formerly arable, with reference to the marker stones mentioned above (T133). 'Burdons' may have been coined as a name to imply that its cultivation was harder work, or less productive, than that of 'Beadons'.

136 Field. (90 B2) All but one of the stones marking out this plot of land have disappeared the one on the south east corner survives. This is inscribed PCL, which stands for Pensford Church Lands, not Publow Church Lands. Dr Joe Bettey has explained that, as in Compton Dando, the distinction between these and Glebe Lands was that the former were to provide income for the maintenance of the Church building, while the latter were to provide the living for the vicar. The surviving stone doesn't look much older than early 19th century, but this could be a replacement for successive markers put in to demarcate a plot originally allocated in the medieval era. Pensford Church Lands paid for the rebuilding of Pensford Church in 1869, [74] but the lands were sold some time after this.

137 Field. (90 B2) as above.

138 Sandhills. (90 B2) Also shown as Sandhills in 1776. Also contains a spring, the source of the brook referred to in T134.

139 Sandhill Close. (90 B2) Sandhill in 1776.

140 Moor Croft. (90 B2) Made from the two fields shown on the 1776 map, both called Mooncroft. The 1806 map shows arable cultivation of the southern half, with the furrows going south west to north east, following or dictating the line of the earlier division between the two halves. The chink in the outline of the north east border of T140 is a typical clue to the previous existence of old arable furlongs, and the 1806 record confirms this. 'Moor' seems to be another example of misreading, for 'Moon'. The 1806 map also says 'Moor Croft' but there is unlikely to have ever been anything moor-like about the field. 'Moon' field names are not uncommon, but are so far unexplained. 'English Field Names' is not very convincing here: 'It may allude to a location favoured for moonlight activities such as poaching'. The EFN definition of a croft: 'small piece of land, frequently attached to a house, and almost invariably enclosed.' Perhaps the name was originally applied to the southern half of T115, which would fit these characteristics. However, they do not appear to apply to two of the other three 'crofts' in Publow - T249 and 346. T305 seems to fit the EFN description. 'Croft' names are sometimes associated with arable use, though all the latter three were pasture in 1839.

141 Upper Sandhills. (90 B2) Shown as Sandhills in 1776. The eastern edge of this

field is about 10ft higher than the level in the adjacent T138, a common characteristic in this parish, where hundreds of years of arable cultivation have shifted the soil downhill. So the eastern edge of T141 has risen and the western edge of T138 has gone down.

T142 Cottage and field. (90 B2) The word 'Harwar' on the 1776 map refers to the tenant Nicholas Harwar.

T143 Field. (90 B3) In 1930 a bronze age arrow head was found in an arable field somewhere near Whitley Batts by Mr F.Baum, and presented to Taunton Museum. [75] Unfortunately there is no record of precisely which field it was found in, but a Roman coin found by Mr Baum was at T63.

T146 House and garden. (90 B3) Focal point of a possible hamlet in Saxon times

T147 Home Close. (90 B3) The ground seems very disturbed here in various places, and may represent the remains of very early mining activity, which would support the suggestion that T147, 148. 149, and 150 were part of a large block of common land up to the 17th or 18th century (see page 2). The lack of distinctive names and their continuing condition of old pasture containing a number of oak trees, adds to that impression.

T149 Hilly Piece. (90 A3) The northern edge is bounded by the only stone wall that has been found in Publow as a field boundary. This might provide the best evidence for trying to put a date to when this block of common land was divided. In places the wall is still in good condition, and may suggest a mid-18th century date.

T150 Whitley. (90 B3) Called Whitley in 1839, as was T148, but T147,148,149 and 150 are all called 'The Close' in 1776, and probably 'Whitley' was applied from the adjacent Long Whitley in the absence of any other name.

T151 Long Whitley. (90 B3) Shown as Long Whitley on the 1776 survey and Bats Whitley on the 1776 map, from the tenant at that time, Mary Batt, of South Leigh Farm. This would suggest that the current name Whitley Batch is an inversion of the old name, but there is a 1770 reference to Whitley Batch - see below T162. The earliest form of Whitley so far found is Whitely, from 1739, see also T162. There is no obvious derivation in white soil, though it might seem relatively so compared to the fairly sharply differentiated very red soil to the east of the A37. Perhaps it was originally 'wheat', and perhaps the shape contains the reverse 's' of an old arable furlong.

T152 House and garden. (90 B3) Now called Turnpike Cottage and altered unrecognisably in the 1990s from the quaint cottage it had prevously been. Although not indicated as Turnpike Cottage on the maps of 1776, 1806 or 1839, the 1817 Ordnance Survey map does show it [A5]. This is the 'Chelwood Gate' referred to above, page 4, presumably instituted as a turnpike some time after 1727. The pond by the main road at the southern edge of the garden in T153 is also the southernmost edge of the parish, and could be a very ancient pond, as it was probably used as a parish boundary marker.

T153 Gallows Close. (90 B3) The field to the south in Chelwood shares this name, so presumably the gallows would have been in the south west corner of T153. There are no clues as to the period over which it was used. The 1776 map shows a pattern of trees which almost certainly would be the relics of an older system of smaller enclosures. One line carries on that of the A37, and if extended goes precisely to Fry's Bottom Lane, in Chelwood, where it continues that direction. The abrupt angle of the existing road at the north west edge of T153 strongly suggests that the Fry's Bottom route was originally more significant. The south west corner of T153 contains the pond referred to above (T152), possibly the feature incorporated into the boundaries with a pre-medieval estate of Chelwood.

T154 Mill Mead. (90 B3) Shown as Mill Meads in 1776, two meadows overlying a probably older pattern of five fields, judging by lines of trees shown on the 1776 map. There is no obvious evidence of a mill here, and the vicinity may have been too much altered for the survival of many archaeological clues. There is a 1554 reference to a mill called 'Wethergroves' which may have been in 'East Chelworth' [76] and perhaps this and 'Mill Mead' are both referring to the same, early corn mill.

T155 Sweetmans. (91 A3) The 1776 survey calls this Pipershill rather than Sweetmans. Sweetmans presumably refers to a previous tenant. No-one of that name was noted in a quick check of the Publow parish records.

T156 Sweetmans. (91 A3) Sweatmans on the 1776 map and survey.

T157 Lower Long Ground. (94 B3) Called Coalpit Ground on the 1776 survey. Local farmer Brian Watson recalls that there were once the remains of three large bell pits in this field. These pits may have been worked in the early or mid 18th century.

T158 Copse. (90 B3) In 1776 called 'Wood'. The geological map of ST66SW shows another old pit remnant here.

T159 Pipers Hill. (90 B3) Given as Pipers Hill but shown on the map as Pipershill. This is similar to 'Peppershells', which is the name of a field in Compton Dando (one which has recently turned into a wood). Perhaps the name did once mean something -rather just meaning it was tenanted by someone called Piper.

T160 Upper Long Ground. (90 B3) In 1776 this was partly Long Ground and partly (Bat's) Long Ground.

T161 Field. (90 B3) Just marked as 'Church' on the 1776 map, and therefore not on the survey. In 1839 this was owned and occupied by Richard Bullock, whose only other two fields in the parish were T136 and 137, also formerly Church Land. These were all still Church Land in 1806 and were presumably sold by the Feoffees of Pensford Church Land some time between 1806 and 1839.

T162 Cottage and yard. (90 B3) Noted as The Meeting on the 1776 survey. Its origins are precisely established in the dissenters' certificate of October 12th 1770:

'We whose names are underwritten are desirous that the new built House at Whitley Batch should be set apart as a place of public worship for a society of protestant Dissenters call'd Presbyterians'. The statement is signed by 16 men, 'with many others'. [77] The building is still called Chapel Cottage, but its life as a chapel did not last long. By 1793 the Publow court papers have an entry: 'We present the meeting house at Whitley Batch to be ruinous and in decay'. [28] Maybe this was because a more convenient site had been found in Pensford itself. In 1790 a dissenters' certificate had been granted to four dissenters 'of the Independent Denomination' to worship in a house in Pensford then occupied by George Hanney [77] In 1776 George Hanney was listed as living at the house where the smith's shop was (see T23). 100 years previously such 'dissent' was illegal, and in 1670 ten Pensford men, along with one from Woollard, one from Publow, one from Chew Magna and two from Whitchurch, were heavily fined for worshipping 'in other manner than according to the liturgies of the Church of England' in Publow. [78] The site may earlier in the 18th century have been part of a strip of roadside 'waste'. In 1739 Edward Popham had given a lease to a 'cottage erected on the wast with outhouses and 1 acre of garden bounded on the west by the Pensford Chelworth Highway and on the East by Whitley Paddock'. [79] Maybe this was the cottage at T144, which still existed in 1885.

T163 Seven Acres. (90 B3) Also shown as Seven Acres in 1776. The name type and the straight lines of the hedges imply a late enclosure, but give no clue as to its former condition. The south east corner rises to the highest point locally, in T165, and so this would be a logical area for the 'Pryor's Hill' mentioned in 1671, to have been. The 'Pryor' name is unexplained: perhaps a surname, or perhaps relating to a monastic institution such as Keynsham Abbey.

T164 Close. (91 A2) In 1776 shown as a different arrangement of fields, titled Mr Broadrip's Limekiln This map also shows lines of trees which probably relate to an earlier field system, and suggests that the whole block of land between Birchwood Lane, the A37, Chelwood and Birchwood may have some common history of early land use. The kiln site would almost certainly have been by Birchwood Lane somewhere, as the 'lime' to be burnt would have to have been brought by horse and cart. This could have been lias limestone from Red Hill (about a mile and a half to the south west) or the area just to the north of Hunstrete. This kiln was presumably being operated by the 1776 tenant, Mr Broadrip, but there is no evidence for the dates of other Publow limekilns at T385, 394 and 393. John Billingsley noted in 1795 that farm limekilns, burning lime to put on lime-deficient soils, were numerous and well built in Somerset: 'their form is that of a French bottle, the height seventeen feet ... its diameter four feet. They are built on the side of a hill'. [80] A good example of a later limekiln which still survives is by Chewton Wood, at ST609548. There are references to lime burning in the Hunstrete Estate accounts for 1826, for example: Richard

Pearce was paid £4.17.6d for burning 194 quarters of lime at 6d per quarter. [49]

T165 Limekiln Ground. (91 A3) As above. The fact that this title was given to 165 rather than 164 in 1839 might be taken to suggest that the kiln site would have been here somewhere rather than by the road in T164. Alternatively, the kiln might already have been long gone in 1839, and the name transferred to the 'wrong' half of the old field.

T166 Birchwood. (91 A3) Shown as 'Batts Birchwoods' on the 1776 map, and 'Birch Wood' on the 1776 survey. In 1672 Sir Francis Popham signed a licence for coal extraction from Burch Wood, and Burchwood Common, and all other wastes in Publow. [81] It's possible that the name Burchwood would have been applied to the whole of the expanse of Lords Wood and the common north of it, at that time. This would make sense of the name Birchwood Lane, which runs through the larger expanse but not near 166 and 167. The Pophams' freeshare (ie, royalty) returns on mines on the Hunstrete estate are recorded for 1705-1710 and show the decline of Birchwood mine with a corresponding growth at Chelwood and Hunstrete mines. [50] Birchwood production in 1705 earnt the Pophams £3.3.0d.35 If the freeshare was one eighth, and the selling price about 3d per bushel (about 1 cwt) the year's production might have been about 100 tons. If the decline from 1705-1710 is projected backwards, production could have been many times this in the 1672-1705 period (note, the figure of £4.3.0d published in 1952 appears to be a mistake). The title Birchwood, already in use in 1672, implies that the birch (Betula pendula) is native here, not planted. Although birch is a typical pioneer species of places like railway lines, with bare stony soil, on the acid soils here, associated with many other ancient woodland indicator species, it seems well established.

T167 Birchwood. (91 A3) Also Birchwood in 1776, as above.

T168 Lower Close. (91 A2) In 1776 shown as part of Mr Broadrips Limekiln, and Mary Batts Lands. The geological map of ST66SW shows three old pits in the field and at least one of them is still very evident as a slight bank running round the perimeter of the old pit. Probably it was worked in the late 17th or early 18th century - see above. The pits are on the eastern edge of the field, by the wood.

T169 House and yard. (91 A2) Just 'Homestead' in 1776, and now called South Leigh Farm - see T122.

T170 Orchard. (91 A2)

T171 Paddock. (91 A2) Part of an enclosure called Wood Close in the 1776 survey. The eastern edge remains irregular, and may represent the limit of clearance of woodland made in the Saxon era. The northern hedge is probably an old one, and the western one was probably a relatively recent one - it has now gone. An anecdotal account by Ros Anstey of a disastrous, but historic, Pensford Ladies Group expedition across an ancient stile here is contained in the Publow Parish Magazine of November 1987. The stile broke under the weight of one unfortunate lady. The remainder of the party ended up being stung by mysterious insects as they battled through the undergrowth of Lords Wood as night began to fall. Sadly, the person held responsible for the slight miscalculations as to route and timing was, er, myself (but, hey, what an adventure!).

T172 Herns. (91 A2) Just shown as 'Church Land' in 1776, and therefore not on the survey. Still owned by the Feoffees of Pensford Church Land in 1839 (see T136 and 161). As above, an irregular outline suggesting assart, clearance of woodland. The name is probably from the OE 'hyrne' - land in an angle or corner. This might support the suggestion that T172 represents a clearance of woodland in the Anglo-Saxon era and a contemporary part of The Lye - see page 1, and T122 etc. Hern or Hurn field names exist in several local parishes, and it would be reasonable to suggest that not all may be particularly old. Hern is also a surname, of course (the last prior of Keynsham Abbey was a William Herne [7] to raise a red herring which may also be applicable to T163).

T173 Lords Wood. (91 A2) Called Lords Wood and Common in 1776. Curiously, no earlier reference to the name has been found. The present wood spans the parishes of Publow, Compton Dando, Chelwood and Marksbury, but much of the woodland in the latter parishes comprises early 19th century plantation. T180 and 182 had also been turned into plantations by 1885. Nevertheless the T173 part of the wood retains many biological indicators of ancient woodland, in particular the range of its bramble species. Early in the last century, the brambles of Lords Wood were recognised by J.W.White as being of great interest and rarity, and are all listed in 'The Bristol Flora' (1912). [19] More recently another expert (Rob Randall) has been studying them and his findings were published in 'The Flora of Bristol Region' (2000). Several scarce species were re-found in the same places described by White. Lords Wood is full of old coal pits and spoil heaps, and a number of these are shown on the geological map for ST66SW.

T174 Coalpit Close. (91 A1) Just shown as Coalpit on the 1776 survey. No clues as to the date of the pit or pits. This block of land east of Birchwood Lane and north of Lords Wood may have been enclosed from the surrounding common land some time from the late 16th to early 18th century. The tenement at T181 was probably the site of the original farmstead, superseded by that at T176 by 1839. That such buildings were exceptionally permitted on land when it was still common is shown by a record of the Quarter Sessions held at Ilchester in April 1637: 'Sir Francis Popham, Kt, Lord of the Manor of Publoe, and the major part of the inhabitants, these being willing and contented, it was ordered that William Price of Publoe aforesaid, Mason, may erect and build him a cottage upon some part of the wast grownd of the said Manor of Publoe'. [82]

This cottage could have been any one of those around the commons at T58 or T274, but equally it might have been the one at T181.

T175 House Close. (91 B1) The Close, in 1776.

T176 House and garden. (91 B1) Just part of The Close in 1776, see above. The house is now known as Birchwood House. This was a farm until relatively recently, and the 1980s occupier, Bill Thompson, remembered such routines as taking the morning's milk by horse and cart up the lane and along the brook, which had a wide, flat bed, into Woollard. It was also his recollection of the site of the Pensford Church Lands stone (see T136) that enabled it to be found again, after it had become lost in a mass of brambles.

T177 Lower Close. (91 B1) Meadow, in 1776.

T178 The Mead. (91 B1) Meadow, in 1776.

T179 Little Close. (91 B1) The Hill, in 1776.

T180 The Hill. (91 B1) The Hill, in 1776 also. This was made into a plantation between 1839 and 1885. Perhaps the steep slopes and acid soil had not proved conducive to good pasture, just as this may have been the original reason for the survival of woodland in T172.

T181 Farmyard. (91 B1) Shown as The Homestead in 1776 - see above T174.

T182 Pond Close. (91 B2) Also shown as Pond Close on the 1776 survey, and was pasture in 1839, but by 1885 was under plantation. See also below.

T183 Old Pond and Paddock. (91 B2) Shown as Great Pond on the 1776 survey. This pond in 1776 covered over 3.5 acres. It was made by damming Candlestick Brook, and the remains of the dam still exist under the plantation. A considerable mass of water was held back by the dam, and water was taken from the north west corner via a stone lined leat some 600 yards north to a wire mill at T187. This system still seems to have been working in 1806, but was evidently defunct by 1839. A very early date has been suggested for this system, but it is unlikely to be earlier than 18th century, and probably represents a response of one of the local metal working firm to excessive use of the Chew by competing mills if one mill wanted to increase its water supply by raising its dam, this could reduce the power available to the mills upstream by increasing the resistance to the flow. The Publow court papers of January 1749 record just such a complaint about the Woollard weirs from the Publow Mills. [4] In 1776 the wire mill was referred to as New Mill, and was tenanted from the Pophams by Tyndall and Company -see T85. T183 is now within the plantation area added to Lords Wood, but the dam and leat are still visible.

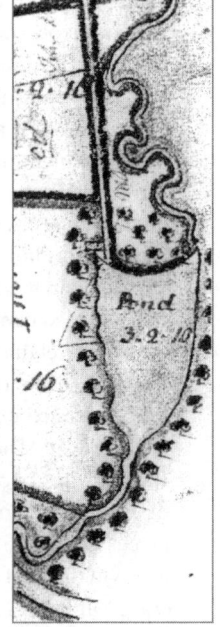

T184 The Mead. (91 B1) Shown as 'meadow' in 1776. Now under plantation.

T185 Lower Mead. (91 B1) 'Meadow' in 1776.

T186 Mill Mead. (89 B2) 'Mill' refers to the one at T187. 'Meadow' in 1776.

T187 Cottage and Gardens. (89 B2) Shown in 1776 as the wire mill referred to above, T183. The building no longer exists, but it looks as if the mill's water wheel may have been on the south side of the building - an overshot wheel with the water then flowing into the brook at the junction of T187 and 188.

T188 Orchard. (89 B2) In 1776 shown as 'a homestead by the mill'. The platform of this building can still be seen in this field.

T189 Cottages and gardens. (89 B2) There is virtually no trace of these cottages, although the line of their back gardens can still be picked out on a 1946 aerial photo. [83] Shown as one cottage in 1776.

T190 Garden. (89 B2) A wild plum tree here by the lane may be the last relic of this. In 1776 there was another cottage here, and the stonework either side of the lane at this point is the only substantial evidence of what must at one time have been a busy industrial hamlet.

T191 Mill Mead. (89 B2) Shown as Mill Mead in 1776. A little bridge aver the leat, probably for farm vehicles and animals can be seen on aerial photos of 1946 etc.[83] There were at one time a number of these bridges.

T192 Great Hill Grounds. (89 B2) Hill Close, or Hilly Ground in 1776. Possible early enclosure from wood pasture, as T133.

T193 Part of the Four Acres. (89 B2) Just 'The Four Acres' in 1776 (part of which was claimed by Mrs ? Jonson).

T194 Stout's Mead. (89 B2) The 1776 map shows the north eastern part of the 1839 field as Stouts. Stout may be from the surname of a pre-1776 tenant, or OE 'ste-ort' 'tongue of land between streams'. [55]

T195 Walls Mead. (89 A2) Also Walls Mead on the 1776 map. Where the name 'walls' occurs, this is often a reference to the remnants of old buildings. It may seem unlikely that a building would have been constructed on a field that probably flooded regularly, but the southern edges are more raised. An aerial photo taken in 1972 suggests a possible building site. [84] A small part of the 1776 Walls Mead had been added to the area of T197, which was laid out some time between 1806 and 1839, see below. The chink in the outline of the eastern boundary of T195 is reminiscent of that in T140, but is unlikely to be related to arable past use in this situation. It is not shown on the 1776 map.

T196 Hill Ground. (89 B2) Shown as Hill. Ground on the 1776 map also. See T192.

T197 Publow Common. (89 A3) The field shown as T107 in 1839 had been made by enclosing the old Publow Common some time between 1806 and 1839. The 1776 map just calls the overall area common, and the word 'coalmine', in conjunction with the compass drawn over the common, has been taken to imply that the whole area was a coalmine. However, it could have just referred to one or two large pits in the south east part of the common. In the 1806 map, the whole expanse of common, which included the subsequently separated T130, 199 and 198, is shown as pasture called Publow Common. The coalmine shown in 1776 was possibly being worked then, or alternatively it might have been the remnant of the old Birchwood Pit (see T166). At any rate it is unlikely to have been extensive, as a regular item in the Publow court papers from at least 1759 to 1786 reads that, anyone putting sheep on Publow Common in the spring or summer would be fined five shillings (the rate went up to 10 shillings in 1786). [28] Presumably no-one would be tempted to send their sheep out onto a coalmine. Since these fines went to the Pophams, doubtless the summer grazing was in some way reserved; in other words, some commons became less 'common' than others before they disappeared altogether. Its 19 acres were described as arable in 1839.

T198 Lye Common. (89 A3) See above and T130. Its 22 acres were arable in 1839.

T199 Lye Common. (89 A3) See above and T130. Its 8 acres were described as arable in 1839.

T200 Bakers Six Acres. (89 A3) Also shown as Bakers on the 1776 map, but listed as Bookhill, tenanted by Mr Baker, on the 1776 survey. The word Bookhill was applied to 201, 202, 203, and 204 in 1839. The 1806 map calls these Brookhill, and also applies that name to most of the field shown as T207 in 1839. Bookhill is the earlier form, and probably closer to the original, for which a variety of unconvincing explanations may be offered: i) perhaps from 'boc', beech tree. Any beech trees in the locality now are probably planted, but there might have been a few indigenous OE 'boc' or 'boec' trees about. ii) perhaps from Willelmo Bokke, mentioned on the Exchequer Lay Subsidy returns for Publow of 1387 iii) from 'bookland', part of common land granted by charter (under sovereign's orders) to a private owner (from another 'boc', meaning a document). iv) from Master John Bokeland, who resigned as Vicar of the chapel of St Thomas the Martyr, Pensford, around the end of the 15th century. [85]

T201 Bakers. (89 A3) Again, Bookhill in 1776. The earlier map is interesting in showing how T200 and 201 were originally separated by a wedge shaped piece of Publow Common. On the west side of this wedge was a trackway leading to the homestead at T205, and thence to Publow. The trace of quite a deep trackway can still be seen here, despite the removal of the hedge between T200 and 201.

T202 and 203 Bookhill. (89 A2) See T200. A dam was built across the north east edge of T203 in the mid-1980s, blocking the spring that runs down from T134, and creating a pool for fishing.

T204 Bookhill Home Mead. (89 A2) The name implies that all the fields named Bookhill may have originally have been farmed from the homestead just visible in this plot on the 1776 map. This tenancy in 1776 was held by a Mr Taylor, and the holding also included most of T207. This homestead seems to have disappeared by 1806.

T205 Cottage and garden. (89 A2) This cottage disappeared between 1839 and 1885. The area between T204 and 205 could be an early settlement site. It is notable that two substantial tracks, one from Pensford Down (T45a) and one from The Lye (T122) lead towards here. Perhaps the track between T86 and 88 also carried on to here.

T206 Orchard. (89 A2)

T207 Bakers and Daffys. (89 A2) The 1806 map shows that hedges on the east side had been knocked out some time between then and 1839 to make T207. In 1776 one little enclosure marked on the map as Baker's was called Price's Paddock (shown as Barken Paddock on the 1806 map), and the other small field shown as 'Flowers' was listed as Drakes Close. However, the major part of T207 was in 1776 shown as Water Meads. Whether this implies any system of water meadows functioning along the lines of the systems used in Hampshire etc, with deliberate flooding of the land, seem doubtful. 'Daffy's' is also applied to T216 and 217. John Field noted that the possessive form normally suggests a surname, but that this is not necessarily the case - 'even clerks writing tithe apportionments seemed to follow the rule - if you see an s put an apostrophe before it'. Daffy is not very likely as a surname, and seems more possible as a word for the wild daffodils which still grow within half a mile of here, but no evidence of this use of such a word has been located so far. Drake's Close was just up the river from Duckpools (T98), 'Ducknest near Publow Bridge' (north west quarter of T98, in 1776), and Henpound (T208), and adjoined Water Meads, so the probability is that Drake is from drake. The surname Drake has not been noted locally. Barken could conceivably be related to bark, or perhaps old tannery pits. There must have been a specific reason for this very unusual small enclosure within the larger riverside ham, not quite abutting the river. Tannery pits existed by T268, although tannery offices were possibly at T232. Tannery pits involved the steeping of hides in the tannic acid obtained from oak bark for a considerable period of time. Objections to the appalling smell this produced figure in the Publow court papers, and this could provide a reason for isolating such pits.

T208 Hen Pound. (89 A2) Also Hen Pound in 1776. See T102.

T209 Mill Cottages and yard. (89 A2) Shown as The Mills in 1776, or Publow mill, listed on the 1776 survey as tenanted by Freeman Esquire and Co. This was the John Freeman and Copper Company, who had also occupied Bye Mills and Pensford Mills from the early 18th century, and who later took over the Woollard rolling mill [62] (T229). The Publow Mill was fed by a leat which is shown on the tithe map running from Publow Bridge across to T209. The bridge also included a weir (of which the Becket Centre had a photograph) which guided the water into the leat. This bridge has keystones signifying rebuilding in 1788 and 1810, the earlier one marked JF & Co. By 1839 the owner of both Publow and Woollard Mills was Richard Bright, the former inhabited by himself and the latter by William Smith.

In April 1759 John Freeman and Co were fined £5 for blocking up the way through the 'Ware Pool', and they were ordered to lay it open again and make it passable. [28] This is puzzling in that implies the existence of a weir but not necessarily of a bridge.

T210 Field. (89 A2) Shown as The Conygear in 1776. See T125. The proximity to Publow Church, with its known links with Keynsham Abbey, make this a strong possibility as an artificially constructed and enclosed medieval rabbit warren. In 1280 the abbott of Keynsham Abbey was given a licence to enclose a pasture called 'Wynterleye' with a wall and make of it a rabbit warren. There are traces of wall by the road edging T212, but these are probably associated with the later farm. However, further investigation would be worthwhile. The 'Wynterleye' is thought to refer to a 'conygre' in Keynsham parish, but there is no evidence to confirm that. Rabbits continued to be an important part of the local economy into the 19th century. In 1713, £6 was received by Alexander Popham for 'Rabbitts in the Park, clear of Expenses' [107] more than the royalty from Birchwood coalmine for 1705 - see T166). The number and value of rabbits from the big warren in Compton Dando parish, just east of Lords Wood, is precisely recorded for the years 1820-1822. From November 1820 to February 1821, 3,304 rabbits were sold to Mr Davies in Bristol, yielding £144 income, minus £1 for 'bad rabbits'. From October 1821 to March 1822 Mr Davies paid a further £102 for another 2,040 rabbits, at 2/- per couple. [86] However, the days of the rabbit had been numbered since 1807, when N.Kent produced a scathing report on the continuing practice of rabbit production from Hunstrete Park and Warren:

'No Plantations can in our opinion be raised, or any beauty effected in the Park to any extent, unless the Rabbits be kept very much under, if not totally destroyed, for their burrowing will not only cause greater deformity, but they will ruin all young plantations that may be made, except that they are protected by walls. And as to profit, we cannot conceive they can produce so much as might be made from the Agistment of Cattle upon an improved Herbage, besides which they must tend to starve the Deer, and all other Cattle that are turned into the Park. We are sensible we give this advice against a strong bias in favor of the Rabbits; but we cannot bring ourselves to recommend a continuance of the present slovenly state of this large tract of land by continuing it in Warren.' [A3]

This advice may finally have been taken in 1822, when the rabbit figures cease, but there is a considerable increase in the income from agistment

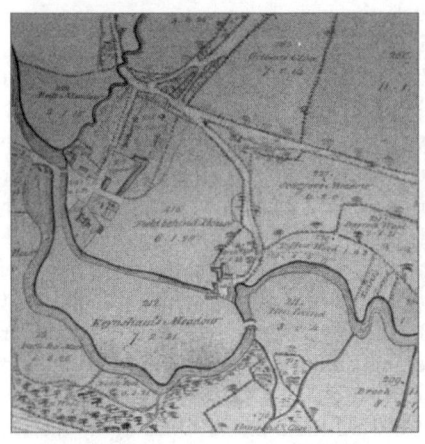

The 1806 map of central Publow

of cattle (taking in livestock and charging for their grazing etc) from 1821 (£32.4.6d) to 1823 (£51.19.3d). [86] The record of payment of £18 in December 1822 for the construction of 180 perch (990 yards) of 4.5 ft high wall in the park may confirm that. [63]

211 House and lawn. (88 B2) Shown as 'Homestead by the church' in 1776. The 1806 survey calls this, or T212, 'A genteel house with large offices, stabling etc and yard'. There is no clue as the age and quality of this house, or the purpose of the offices, but by 1873 the site was described as 'yard with ruinous buildings'. In 1873 the site was exchanged by Francis Leyborne Popham (see T97, 217 and 265) for three fields. The Reverend A.Bellamy thereby obtained the site on which to build the present building on the site - initially the parsonage, now a private house. [87]

T212 Yard, garden and orchard. (88 B2) In 1776 Mr Owen tenanted the 'Homestead by the Church', and his holding was the most compact in the parish, comprising 89 acres of the central part of Publow, plus lands in Charlton field (see page 2. Part of Charlton field is shown in the north east corner of the Publow map). This holding was the second largest in Publow in 1776, and its central position would suggest it as the demesne farm, but unfortunately there is no evidence of any Publow lord ever having lived here. Neither is there any evidence of any continuity in the past of this holding as one unit.

T215 Seagrove. (89 A2) Also Seagrove in 1776. It had been suggested that the Sea-element might be derived from OE 'secg', (= sedge) but John Field commented: 'This would not be likely to give a long 'e' as in 'seal, or a hard 'g' ... A surname possibility once again, or unrecognisable first element combining with -grove'. The situation next to Seagrove Brake, and the several other 'grove' names for woods in the parish (see T111) probably support the latter suggestion.

T216 Daffy's Mead. (89 A2) Also Daffy's Mead in 1776, when the 'Sir Charles' shown on the map referred to Sir Charles Taint, see T293, and the introductory section on 'Ownership'.

T217 Daffy's Mead. (89 A2) As above, see also T207 and 211.

T218 Seagrove Brake. (89 A2) In 1776, three divisions in the wood can be seen. The western part is described as 'wood adjoining Seagrove', the middle part as 'the Brake by the Copper mills' and the eastern part as 'the Brake'. The western and eastern parts were tenanted by Mr Owen (see T212) and middle part by Mr Cottle (see T301), the two largest landholders in the parish, and this may indicate the value of the wood. As suggested above (T111), there may have been a lot of trees and wood pasture in the parish, but not many areas where animals were excluded and from which a supply of underwood could be obtained. The area now has an open wood-pasture type of character similar to those which have developed in T210, but at one time might have retained some of the characteristic species of ancient woodland which still survive nearby, such as wild daffodil.

Large numbers of navelwort (Umbilicus rupestris) grow on rocky areas in this wood, but in no other local wood.

T219 Ham. (89 A2) On the 1776 map, all four enclosures subsequently covered by T219 and T220 are just noted as The Mountain. The gradient is not particularly steep or high here, so perhaps the title is an ironic one. The hedges shown on the 1776 map look straight and relatively recent, and might have been an imposition on a large expanse of grazing such as is shown around Parsonage Farm (T10). Jenny Scherr has speculated as to whether the title could have referred to some raised feature, no longer extant. A barrow? T219 is shown as Mill Ham in 1806 (for 'ham', see T14).

T220 The Mountain. (89 A2) As above. This field occupies a space between two areas of sandstone, and so probably has less acid soil than some of the fields around it.

T224 Cottage and garden. (87 B3) See the map of Woollard opposite. The cottage was occupied by Mary Bryant in 1839.

T228 Field. (89 B2) Shown as arable in 1839. In 1776 shown as an orchard.

T229 Mill Cottages and yard. (89 B2) The 1806 map indicates that the weir was probably along the line of the remains of the little footbridge there. See T85, 183 and 209. Since the publication of 'Publow Field Names' in 1988, some very dubious theories have been advanced suggesting a pre-18th century origin for this bridge. As the previous book suggested, the bridge's origin was likely to be with the 18th century mill at Woollard. It could have been similar to the little footbridge which survives at Pensford next to the site of the old mill, and was under the same ownership. The bridge could have provided a short cut to Birchwood Lane to and from the mill, but it would have made no sense in any known medieval route, and has no visible medieval features.

The old footbridge by the mill at Woollard photographed by H.S.Thompson in 1928

` A 1999 report by Bath and North East Somerset Council's Archaeologist Bob Sydes concluded: 'The main clue to its date is the bridge's association with a stone weir and mill race for Woollard Mill on the north bank. This mill was converted from a water powered Grist Mill (corn grinding) to a Rolling Mill for the production of tin plate in 1730, and it is extremely likely that the weir and bridge were constructed at around this time. It is highly unlikely to have been constructed earlier.' The new footbridge nearby was constructed in 2001.

T231 Bell Inn. (87 B3) This is not listed on the 1776 map or survey: it is shown as number 110, but presumably was not owned by the Pophams at that time. It is on

Woollard's medieval bridge, demolished after the 1968 floods, and the old chapel behind. Photographed by H.S.Thompson in November 1928.

the 1806 survey as The Bell Inn. Note, this is the building in the photograph above, on the south of the road, not the one on the north (T232) which subsequently acquired the sign and title of Bell Inn. It is now called Newbridge House. The building at T231 probably originated as a chapel: the photo shows a medieval gable window about 13 foot high, in the east wall of the building. This implies that the original building was open to the roof. The upper floor was inserted 'not later than the early 16C' - Commander E.H.D.Williams. [88] By the time of the Tithe Map of 1839, it was owned by Edward Popham, and tenanted by William Hodges. Incidentally, an article in Bristol and Avon Archaeology 15 (1999) incorrectly states that the Tithe schedule records the property as 'Cottage and Garden'. The article's accompanying plan, which purports to be a detail of the 1839 Tithe map, is actually an attempted drawn copy which wrongly labels T232 as T252 and omits T231 altogether, thereby wrongly implying that it is T224. The article suggests that this could be the chapel mentioned by Collinson as a chantry chapel established by one of the St Loe family. It also suggests the chapel gained significance from its position on a route along the Chew Valley, but, although the bridge was used by modern car travellers (until the bridge's destruction after the flood of 1968) for travelling up the valley to Keynsham, medieval travellers could have been more likely to use the more direct route along Smallbrook Lane. This

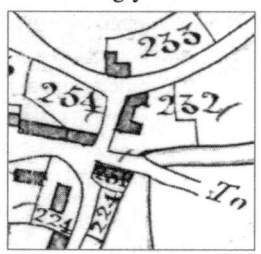

Tithe map, 1839, the centre of Woollard

T232, the house opposite Woollard's former medieval chapel building. It was known as 'The Priest's House' at the time of this 1864 painting

is a green lane which runs from behind T232, which formerly provided a much shorter route to Chewton Keynsham, without needing to cross the Chew. A section of about 500 yards beyond Knowle Farm, in Compton Dando parish, which is now just a foopath was described as the 'old deserted road' in 1758, but in earlier days it would have completed a direct road from Woollard to Keynsham. Woollard's medieval bridge might have been more significant to earlier travellers on north-south routes, connecting to the roads to Hunstrete (as noted earlier, owned by Glastonbury Abbey from the Saxon era until the 16th century) or Birchwood Lane. None of the routes involved the lane by the side of Newbridge House, leading to the much later footbridge by the mill, so the chapel was not sited on a true crossroads.

232 House and orchard. (87 B3) Shown as The Tanyard in 1776, and as 'House, stable and Tanning office' in 1806. In a watercolour of 1864 by W.W.Wheatley (see page 64), the building is referred to as the Priest's House. [89] In 1839 it is just noted as 'House and Orchard', owned by Popham and tenanted by James Weeks. At some point after 1864 it took over the title of Bell Inn. Commander Williams notes that its external details show it to be of late medieval origin, which was confirmed by a more recent survey. This may again have been a product of Keynsham Abbey, and these buildings would have marked a significant boundary of their huge estate - the other side of the old bridge was, and still is, the parish of Compton Dando, which was held by the Bishop of Bath and Wells in the thirteenth century, and had other links with Bath. Keynsham Abbey is known to have had a tannery (at least one record, from 1353). [32] It was repeatedly said in

the 1980s that the Carthusians ran The Old Tannery over the road in the part of Woollard in Compton Dando parish, but there does not appear to be any evidence to support this suggestion (Keynsham Abbey was Augustinian, and in any case did not hold Compton Dando). However, there is evidence that a tannery was run by a Cornelius Duckett in 1732 - he was presented at Publow court for 'throwing his Tann soyle into the streete at Woollard, being very offensive in the footroad and in all the neighbourhood'. [28] There was another tannery in the parish somewhere near T272, T268 etc. There was a Duckett family in Woollard in 1901, and residing at this property, the 'Priest's House'. The Census record suggests that Miriam Duckett (33, born in Wales) was running a small bakery there as well as bringing up a young family, with her husband William Duckett (69, born in Compton Dando).

T234 Orchard. (87 B3)

T235 Lower Mead. (87 B3) In 1776 there was an orchard in the eastern part of Lower Mead.

T236 House and garden. (87 B3) The 1776 tenant was Mr Langford, and the farm is now called Langford's Farm.

T237 Mead. (87 B3)

T238 Great Broomy. (87 B3) Between 1776 and 1806 the fields were altered to the pattern shown in 1839. In 1776 two closes were called Great Broomey close. Broom (Cytisus scoparius) still grows naturally in old pastures in this parish, generally those too steep to be easily accessible to tractors, and on acid soils, often associated with sandstone. It can be taken to indicate a soil pH of between 3.5-6.5, and can also tolerate very poor soils. The name therefore implies lateish enclosure of poor pasture, but the area might have been arabally cultivated before such pasture developed.

T239 Little Ground. (87 B3) Also shown as Little Ground in 1806, but part of a field called seven Acres in 1776.

T240 Upper piece. (87 B3) Arable in 1839. In 1776 comprising two fields - Little Ground and one of the Great Broomey Closes.

T241 Magnet. (87 B3) Just shown as Glebe land in 1776 - the 1776 map did not list details of this as it belonged to the vicar rather than to the Pophams (see T10). The shape suggests a section within a larger arable field, and may have been allocated as such in the medieval era. Different sections within arable fields did occasionally have their own names, and this could also be a medieval name. Glebe terriers survive for most local parishes, listing the names of Glebe lands and brief descriptions of them. None have survived for Publow, so no earlier form of 'magnet' has been found. Perhaps from something like 'magna', for the largest section in the field.

T242 Long Mead. (87 B3)

T244 Bristol Mead. (87 B3) Also Bristol Mead in 1776. By the the road to Bristol from Woollard, a possible derivation.

T245 Barn Close. (87 B3) Barn Close on the 1776 map, but shown as Barn Mead on the 1776 survey. Possibly from the building on the southern edge of the close.

T246 Publow Hill. (87 A3) Also shown as Publows Hill in 1776 - note this is not the area shown as Publow Hill on the 1885 OS map, and subsequent OS maps. The 1885 map also shows an odd feature in the field, which looks like an old quarry or pond.

T247 Orchard. (87 A3) Very different in 1776, when the settlement pattern seems similar to that at T45a (Pensford Down), encroaching cottages making the outline of the remaining common land concave, or funnel-shaped, matching the description of common land noted by Oliver Rackham: 'A common proclaims itself as the piece of land left over after all the private land has been hedged. Roadside verges are an extension of the common, although gates or 'hatches' often stood in the mouths of the funnels'. [17] Such a gate is shown where the 'funnel' joins the road at the eastern edge of Priest Down. The strip of land shown as 'In hand' is described on the survey as 'An orchard by Pine's House', but looks like a relatively recent enclosure from the common. Pine's House and the adjoining plots (marked 'Crasy', possibly once containing a cottage) might then have been set within the common, much as the block T66, 67, and 68 were. Clearly the main track could also have passed through this strip, and then been diverted round Pine's house to the road's present route.

T248 Cottages and gardens. (87 A3) Just called 'cottage' in 1776, tenanted by James Pine, hence the earlier reference to Pine's House.

T249 Purnells Croft. (87 A3) Just 'Glebe' on the 1776 map. See T10 (Glebe) and 140 (Croft).

T250 Lower Publow Hill. (87 A3) The 1776 map seems particularly carelessly drawn here, as various straight lines of hedges appear from the 1806 map very unlikely to have been straight in 1776. The 1806 map shows all the hedges as fairly wavy in outline, and hence probably early - perhaps early 16th century. The 1776 map calls part Publows Hill and part 'A Close'. The part of 'A Close' added to the larger field was added by altering the line of a hedge between 1776 and 1806. The recent Ordnance Survey Pathfinder map had 'Priest Down' written over this area. This has led to speculation that this may be the area where John Wesley (1703-91) preached - he had to preach in the open air as he was banned from preaching in churches. But, this is not Priest Down - see T274. On one visit in 1742, Wesley had to be rescued from a hostile mob after someone turned a bull loose in the field where he and his followers were.

T251 Two strips. (87 A3) Not specifically shown in 1776, probably because it was discounted as roadside 'waste'. The total of 'Streets, Roads, Lanes Etc' in the 1776 survey was 30 acres, and would have included many such wide verges. This kind of encroachment, where undertaken without the consent of the lord of the manor, or the community generally, was called purpresture. The practice still happens, when the community or parish council fails to notice or raise any objection.

T252 Orchard. (87 B3) 'A Close' in 1776.

T253 Cottages and gardens. (87 B3) In 1776 a part of these was referred to on the survey as 'pt of Paradise Row', although the writing here is a pencil addition, not necessarily contemporary. The building in 1776 seems to comprise one block by the Publow Road and another by the road to Keynsham. By 1806 this had become a block of four cottages by the Publow Road, with another block of two cottages set back slightly to the west. This rebuilding presumably happened in 1782, the date on the date stone (the similarity in the date stone to that at Greens Folly, Pensford, suggests a similar history of ownership by people connected with local mills - seeT85). The same building lay-out is shown on the 1839 map, but by 1885 the most recent block of two cottages had been demolished and replaced by a further block of four cottages, making a total of eight. 'Paradise' could signify good or poor land (irony), or 'paradise' seed used in late medieval times. [55]

T254 see above. (87 B3)

T255 see above. (87 B3)

T256 Orchard. (87 B3)

T259 Barn Close. (87 A3) Just 'A Close' in 1776, but shown containing a building which was presumably a barn.

T260 Barretts Close. (87 A3) In 1776 listed as Barriots Close.

T261 Broad Field. (87 A3) In 1776 shown as Broad Fold, containing a large number of trees. The hedge to the west of this field is the only surviving part of the hedge shown in 1776 as a continuous line from the Publow Road up to the road to Bristol. The 1806 map also suggests that it was planted as one line, but gives few clues as to the date.

T262 Gilbert Close and Waste. (87 A3) The waste referred to can be seen as part of a strip running down the west of T262, and possibly indicated by a line of trees an the 1776 map. This waste would have been an extension of the Priest Down Common (T214) - see T247. Perhaps the hedge on the east of T262 was an earlier limit of Priest Down Common, and the hedge on the west a later boundary, showing further encroachment. The final encroachment and privatisation of even these roadside strips can be seen on the 1839 map - see T251.

T264 Garden. (87 A3) See above.

T265 Garden (87 A3). This looks like another strip of waste, but there is now a slightly wider paddock at this point. In 1873 it was one of the plots given by the Rev A.Bellamy to Francis Leyborne Popham in an exchange deal - see T211.

T266 Garden. (87 A3) Shown on page 1 of the 1776 survey as 'A Cottage and Garden above Publow Church', at the time 'in hand', ie not tenanted. The 1806 map shows two plots within this, with possibly a small building in each. This or

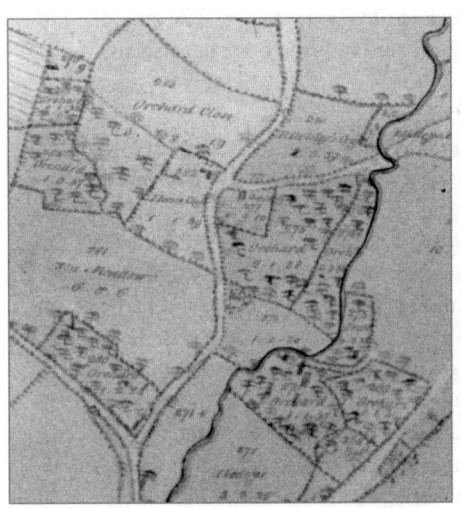

Signs of medieval occupation just north of Publow, on the 1806 map. There were tannery pits here - see T268 etc

these building(s) had gone by 1839, and there was no building here in 1885 either. The bungalow now on the site is not shown on the 1946 aerial photographs, and was probably built shortly after this.

T267 Cottage and garden. (88 B1)

T268 Hedge Mead. (88 B1) Listed as 'A Close By The Tannery Pits' in 1776. 'Hedge' is probably derived from the 1776 tenant Hedges. The tannery pits were probably close to water, which suggests they were probably in T272, see below.

T270 Cottage and orchard. (88 B1) The 1806 map shows a building between this plot and the one to the north, probably a cottage in two halves. The 1776 map shows a further cottage here. All three had gone by 1885.

T271 see above.

T272 House, yard and orchard. (88 B1) On the 1806 map six buildings are shown in the lower part of this enclosure. The 1776 map is less clear, but various buildings here are not specified and so may have been non-Popham dwellings or tannery buildings. Perhaps the offices referred to at 211 or 212 could have related to a tannery here. Tanners were, in the 16th and 17th century, regarded as being of fairly high status - John Locke's mother Agnes Keene was the daughter of a Wrington tanner, and other members of the Locke family married Keenes. At any rate, by 1871 just three buildings were shown here, and by 1885 they all seem to have gone. The access to these buildings was by the little track from T274. The curved shape of this track is preserved in the present right of way, which unfortunately was very overgrown and obstructed in the 1980s. The track is quite deep, which suggests either medieval or pre-medieval origins for the buildings here. Or alternatively it could have been worn down by heavy cart loads of hides for the tan pits.

T273 Orchard. (88 B1) Shown as containing a building in 1776 and 1806.

T274 Pris Down. (88 B1) Shown as Priest Down on the 1776 and later maps, but not named on the 1806 map. The earliest known form is Priest Down, from John Wesley's journal, May 7th 1739. In 1739 Wesley recorded that he preached every other Thursday 'near Pensford', probably again at Priest Down, though he also preached in at least one house in Pensford, in 1760 (see also T20 and T250).

Jenny Scherr has pointed out that Pris, the 1839 description on the Tithe schedule, could actually be the earlier form - from the Old Welsh 'prisc' or 'prysg', meaning copse or thicket (this is the probable derivation of Priston). Various encroachments on the common reduced the acreage recorded in 1776 from 14.2.8 acres to 9.2.13 in 1839, by which time it was no longer common land. The characteristic funnelling into the entrance from the east has already been noted (see T247), but a similar pattern can be seen to the west, where it is joined by the hollow way, between T305 and T274. This would suggest that T306 was also a relatively late encroachment from the common, and the main purpose of the hollow way was as a route for livestock to and from the common. A similar funnelling might be implied at the south, where the hedge goes southwards from T273, which would imply the plots at 269, 270 and 271 might be later encroachment. Another 18th century reference is to 'Priest Down', the Publow Court papers recording a reference to clay holes lately made there. [28] In 1839 the area is shown as arable, but despite that some old grassland indicator species have survived, for example Dyer's Greenweed (Genista tinctoria).

T275 Orchard. (88 B1) In 1776 this was 'a Close' and in 1806 'An Orchard Called Rowleys'.

T276 Cottages and gardens. (88 B1) This pair of 17th century cottages is now Listed.

T277 Cottage. (88 B1) Possibly two cottages here in 1776, but one in 1806. The same little enclosure and one or two buildings are also shown on the 1885 OS map, but these had gone by 1911.

T278 Orchard. (88 B1) In 1776 the map shows a close marked with distinctive but unexplained splodges. This is probably what is referred to on page 19 of the 1776 survey as 'A Homestead called Rowlers'. The name Rowleys could subsequently have been applied to T275 as by 1806 part of this close had been incorporated into it. This close could possibly have contained the tannery pits referred to above, see T268.

T279 Hedges's. (88 B1) In 1776 'By Hedges', both referring to the 1776 tenant.

T281 Close. (88 B1) Incorporating the 1776 'Mead' and 'Four Acres'. The hedges had been taken out by 1806, but

The Publow Oak, in T281

one ancient oak remains. This tree, now known as 'The Publow Oak', is over 32 foot in circumference (at five foot above ground) and possibly the sixth biggest in England. In the opinion of the late Alan Mitchell, the veteran tree expert, it could be over 500 years old. There are a couple of good anecdotes about this tree in 'The Natural History of the Chew Valley' (1987), one involving Pensford's most famous living resident, Acker Bilk.

T282 House, yards and orchard. (88 B1) On the 1817 OS map, this is shown as Hermitage Farm (see T298). Now known as Publow Farm. A cart shed here was surveyed in 2000 prior to its conversion to a dwelling, and it was found to contain an 'unnecessarily' complex roof structure, probably 17th century, hinting at some possibly unrecognised special function, or roof beams imported from an earlier building. [109]

T283 Home Close. (88 B1) In 1776 the northern part was 'A Close' and the southern part was part of a four acre orchard.

T284 Garden. (88 B1) The same enclosure shown on the 1776 and 1806 maps. Plots this small usually only exist as the curtilage of a dwelling. Perhaps T284 originated this way.

T285 Three Acres. (88 B1) In 1776 and 1806 the eastern part of this was a small orchard. In 1806 the remainder of the field was arable, but in 1839 it was pasture.

T286 Paddock. (88 B1) In 1776 another small orchard.

T287 Summer Leaze. (88 B1) In 1776 called Summer Leys.

T288 Butts orchard. (88 A1) Not specified on the 1776 survey as it belonged to Sir Charles Taint. In 1911 this was Lot 2 in the first major sale of the Pophams' Hunstrete Estate land. It was sold as a piece of 'Building Land' of 1 acre 2 rods and 14 perches, and was bought for £140 (£88 per acre).

T289 Butts. (88 A1) In 1776 just marked as Glebe Land (see T7-10 and T11). Shown as an orchard in 1885, and continuing us such until 1987 when it was grubbed up.

T290 Rush Mead. (88 A1) The 1776 map included this in The Butts, and shows two sections within the field. The 1806 shows the northern of these as Butt Piece and the smaller southern piece (1.3.0 arp) as Rush Mead. In 1738 this was let to John Fifoot of Stanton Drew, and in 1758 it was let to Martha Fifoot (the reference is to a one and a half acre Rush Mead, presumably the same one). [90] The Butts title and field shape suggest that it was part of an open field in the early medieval era, but the 'Rush' suggests that it subsequently became poor, badly drained pasture.

T291 Four Acres. (88 A1) Also Four Acres in 1776.

T292 Close. (88 A1) The Close in 1776.

T293 Piece. (86 B3) The area covered by T293 to 299 is absent from the 1776 map as it was owned by Sir Charles Taint. The Tynte family had a lot of land in North Somerset, and detailed rentals for their properties in Pensford (ie the non-Publow part) exist for 1659 and 1730. [91] This block of land, together with all the other lands owed by Sir Charles in 1776, as well as some owned by Lord Paulet in 1776, were owned by William Lloyd in 1839.

T294 Orchard. (86 B3) This is shown on a map of Sir Charles Taint's lands dated about 1770, and is titled Little Amercam. [92] Amercombe House, about 300 yards north west of here, is shown as Amercombe Cottage on the 1817 OS map. There is no obvious combe (valley) here that could be referred to, unless it is the shallow vales running along to the west of T349 or north of 295. Among numerous possible derivations of the Amer element is perhaps one in common with Hammerhill Wood, about a mile to the west. If Hammer Hill referred to the plateau hill between the two points, a similar name might have been applied to the east as to the west. Again, the small size of T294 implies a possible former curtilage. Mary Gelling's opinion on the derivation of the 'Amer' in Amersham (Buckinghamshire) is from a personal name - Ealhmund, and that the 'ham' in that regional context probably indicates an early Saxon settlement. [93]

T295 Side Long. (86 B3) In the 1776 map, this is shown as two fields, Little Sideland and Great Sideland. Side could refer to side of the homestead at T298, or the side of the brook running along the north of T295. Or, if an older name, from OE 'sid', ie spacious or broad.

T296 Corn Leaze. (86 B3) Not on the c1770 map (see T294), or the 1776 or 1806 Popham maps.

T297 Home Mead. (86 B3) Also Home Mead on the c1770 map.

T298 Orchard and Barton. (86 B3) On the c1770 map as House, Garden and Orchard. A building and lines representing possible divisions within a garden and yard are shown on the 1885 map, by which time the GWR line had been built immediately to the west. By 1911 the Hunstrete Sale map shows that T295, 298, 299, 297 and possibly part of 296 on the eastern side of the railway line had been made into one field. Vivian Ritson's 'History of Pensford and Publow' (1913) describes this field as containing the site of the hermitage established by Gilbert de Clare c1228, 'now marked by a ruinous stone shed', probably the building shown on the 1885 map. However, this traditional view should not be assumed to be correct - excavation of the site might be needed to confirm it. At Taunton there is a 16th century deed, in Latin, referring to the feoffment of 'the hermitage called Clarelew' and other documents relating to it. [94] The record of the hermitage being established here in 1228 suggests that 1) if the site was referred to as Publow, then the parish boundary shown in 1776 may have been established by 1228, and 2) to be suitable for a hermitage, this was one of the wildest, least populous or cultivated areas within the Keynsham Abbey lands, excluding Fillwood Chase (preserved for hunting - see T387).

T299 Coalpit Close. (86 B3) In c1770, this was two enclosures - the southern half called Coalpit Close, and the northern half Common. The fragment of common, nearly two and a quarter acres, seems significant, especially since T300 was also called Coalpit Close, and coal pits are frequently associated with old common land (see T166). At the time the hermitage was established this may well have been part of a large, continuous waste or common, including that of Priest Down etc (T274).

T300 Coalpit Close. (86 B3) Shown as Coalpit in 1776, and in 1806 as Coalpit Closes, a hedge dividing the field in two.

T301 House, Yard and Garden. (86 B2) In 1776, The Homestead, tenanted by Mr Cottle, hence the current name Cottles Farm (see also T218). The 1817 OS map refers to this farm as Carsbrook (or possibly Garsbrook, the reprint is not clear), presumably from the brook running past it, from Newbarn Farm to the Chew by Publow, Bridge. An undated map in Bristol Record office, probably mid-19th century, calls the eastern extension of Ringspit Lane 'Lane leading to Casebrook', [95] probably referring to the lane's ford over the brook between T360 and 350. Probably from OE 'caers' = cress. [55]

T302 Orchards. (87 A2) Shown as two closes on the 1776 map, and as two orchards on the 1806 map, the Wansdyke crossing the northern orchard. The hedge dividing the two orchards overlays another smaller enclosure by the brook.

T303 Gorse. (87 A2) Called The Grove on the 1776 and 1806 maps, which (see T111) may imply late wood pasture, and previous common grazing status. Gorse also implies slightly acid rough pasture surviving to 1839.

T304 Lower Coalpit Close. (87 A3) Just called Lower Close in 1776 and 1806. An old coal pit is shown in the north west corner of this field on the geological map for ST66SW.

T305 Hickley's Croft. (87 A3) Shown as Ketcheys on the 1776 map, and Ritchlay's Croft on the 1806 map. Three names seemingly having little in common, yet all possibly deriving from the same unknown origin, apparently distorted by misreading rather than mishearing. Badly written H's, K's and R's can all look similar. See also T140 and 274. Perhaps from Hick and -ley (see page 19, and T306). The 1806 map shows a small enclosure by the brook similar to that in T302.

T306 Hedges's Long Ground. (87 A3) Called Hedges Long Ground In 1776 and 1806. The 1806 map shows the southern and eastern hedges to be straight but the northern and western hedges to be irregular, suggesting that the straight hedges might have been 18th century, to take another 3.25 acres out of Priest Down Common.

T307 Lime Close. (87 A3) Glebe land, and so not named on the 1776 and 1806 maps. The local geology map shows the field to be loamy clay, with two sandstone bands surfacing, which implies that the lime needed to be added rather than that it was already there. The definition of Lime Close in English Field Names: 'land to which lime has been applied'.

T308 Holkham. (87 A3) Shown as Hawkham on the 1776 and 1806 maps. Jenny Scherr suggests 'hole' (OE - hollow) if any nearby feature could be so described.

This could possibly apply to the steep little valley made by the brook coming down from the east. Until the early 1980s most of this field was botanically extremely rich, combining species of ancient pasture with woodland species, suggesting ancient wood pasture. In 1984 most of the field was arabalised and the remainder ceased to be grazed, which means the old grassland species are being killed by scrub and bracken. Taken with the slight evidence of either past common status or past wood pasture status in T299, 300, 303, 304, 306 and 309, it seems reasonable to suggest all these areas might have formed one continuous block of common pasture or wood pasture, including Priest Down, up until about the 16th century, perhaps later.

T308a Gt Lime Close. (87 A2) See T307.

T309 Petty Close. (87 A2) Also shown as Petty Close on the 1776 map, although the field acquired part of that to the east between 1776 and 1806. Possibly a surname derivation, but i) the name Petty has not been noted locally ii) there is no apostrophe 's' iii) there is a Pitty Close in Chelwood next to a Coalpit Ground. As T309 is surrounded by 'pit' names, eg 300, 304, 341, 342, this is probably another one.

T310 Field. (87 A2) Probably Glebe Land, but the 1776 and 1806 maps are not too clear on that. There certainly seems to be some alteration between 1776 and 1806, where it looks as if the northern part of a 14 acre block of Glebe land has been split three ways between the three biggest local landowners: Popham, the Church and the Dickinson Estate (in 1769 Edward Popham sold the Popham's Queen Charlton estate to Vickris Dickinson. [96] By 1839, 99 acres of Dickinson's Publow lands had passed to John Gales).

T311 Long Lime Close. (87 A2) Glebe, see T307.

T312 Upper Lime Close. (87 A2) Glebe, see T307.

T313 Sage's Vineyard. (87 A2) Shown as Henry Sage's Vineyards in 1776, and as Sage's Vineyards on the 1806 map, which also shows that the central point where three fields of that name (T313, 314 and 315) converge is the source of the spring leading down past Hawkham to Carsbrook. Henry Sage was the landlord of the King's Arms in Pensford, see T18, so it's not impossible that this was still a functioning vineyard in 1776. The Victoria County History of Somerset notes: 'As late as 1805, there were vineyards at Claverton, £28 having been paid by Richard Holder, who bought the Vineyards Farm in 1701 for four hogsheads of wine from the same'. [97] However, the more likely explanation is that the name was a carry-over from the medieval era, when Keynsham Abbey almost certainly established a large vineyard here on the hill above T313. The first record of vineyards in Somerset is from the 10th century, from Glastonbury Abbey.[98] Keynsham Abbey probably had several vineyards, and one reference to them comes from 1353 when Bishop Ralph complained about the lack of proper accounts of income and expenditure for the vineyards.[32]

T314-315 as above. (87 A3)

T316 Wood. (87 B2) Shown as Capell on the 1776 map, and omitted from the 1806 map. As suggested on page 3, perhaps the Abbey had a building on this spot, a barton or a chapel. Collinson stated in 1791: 'There formerly stood a chapel at a place called Borough-Bank, [Pensford], which was demolished in the middle of the last century, and its materials appropriated to some private use. There had been a chantry founded by the one of the St Loes'. [99] Although the description implies that both chapels were actually in the village of Pensford, there's no evidence to confirm that they were, and as noted earlier, the St Loes chapel might have been the one at Woollard, T231. 'Borough' obviously can't be taken as evidence for an urban setting, as Pensford wasn't a borough. The word could just as likely be taken from the OE 'beorg', a hill or tumulus. Gelling and Cole note that 'a hill called beorg might have a single farm or might be the site of a church'. If, as suggested earlier, the name Publow is partly derived from a no longer extant tumulus, this might be a clue as to roughly where it might have been.

T317 Paddock. (87 B2) Probably included within Capell on the 1776 map.

T318-324 Winyards Hill. (87 B2) Not specified on the 1776 and 1806 surveys as it was not Popham land. Winyard is from vineyard. see T313. The 1776 map marks this as 'Dickinson the Hill', from Vickris Dickinson, see T310. The 1885 and subsequent OS maps note this as Publow Hill, but as noted above, this should apply to T246. It was probably referred to as Winyards, or as The Hill. See also page 3.

T325 Plantation. (87 B2) Again this is not shown on the 1776 or 1806 maps, as it was not Popham land. The plantation could have been partly intended as a boundary marker, as it marks the edge of the block of strips held by Dickinson, then John Gales. The plot is shown as clear of trees in 1885.

T326 Hix's Paddock. (87 A2) As above, not on the 1776 or 1806 surveys. There are five Hick or Hix names, covering an area from here to T339: the others are T334 (Hix's Mead), T335 (At the Hick Meads), T338 (Hick Meads), and T339 (At the Hick Mead), the last three named only appearing as Hick or Hix on the 1776 survey. See also T305 (Hickley). The most obvious derivation would be a surname, but 1) there is a large area, possibly formerly an open field involved 2) Hick or The Hick is not possessive 3) there are Hick names in Compton Dando (Hick Meadow and Hick's Lay) and possibly other local parishes. The 1806 map also shows T337 and 329 as Hicks Meadow and Hick Meadow, respectively, and the likelihood is that the whole block between these names was at one time referred to as Hick or Hix. The shape of the fields looks derived from medieval open field cultivation and in 1839 most of these fields were arable, so the 'mead' and 'meadow' suffixes were from earlier or later phases of land use. See page 17 'The Hwicce'.

T327 Lower Field. (87 A2) In 1806 shown as Bottom Piece, and in 1776 as Cuckow

Slait. Cuckow, or cuckoo, could imply that crops grew earlier or better here than in other sections of the field. Slait names occur in Chew Magna, Stanton Drew and Compton Dando and once referred to extensive areas of grazing, usually by sheep. The derivation is OE ('slaet' or 'sloeget') and the name may also have been applied continuously since Saxon times. On the other hand the continuing use of the word in later centuries suggests that it might also have been applied to grazing created by forest clearance in the medieval era. It is possible that this 'slait' name was the last remnant of a large area once known as 'slait', just as only two Hix names survived to 1839. See also T328 and 329. Michael Costen, writing of the period 700-900AD: 'Field-names of the type sleight, (Old English slact, 'a sheep pasture'), in Stanton Drew, and Chew Magna point to areas of grazing which were extensive. Such areas were important in giving open land on hill-tops and probably on steep slopes also, and were a significant element in the land-use pattern.' So this area could have been pasture in the late Saxon era, coming under the plough by the early medieval era.

T328 Upper Field. (87 A2) Shown as Cuckow Slait in 1776, and Lime Piece in 1806.

T329 Cuckoo Sleight. (87 A2) Shown as Cuckow Slait in 1776, but as Hick Meadow in 1806.

T330 Lime Pits. (87 A2) Glebe land, and so excluded from the 1776 and 1806 surveys. The geological map shows this to be within an area of 'hummocky slips' from the white and blue lias plateau above.[A12] Perhaps these landslips provided enough liassic limestone to be worth excavating, or perhaps the 'pits' refers to the natural hummocks etc. Between 1776 and 1839 this strip had come under the ownership of William Lloyd, and this may have been the Daubenys' first experiment with privatising Glebe Land (see T7 and 310).

T331 Winyards. (87 A2) Glebe land. See T313 and 318.

T332 Woollard Hill. (87 A2) This strip of 1.0.8 arp was acquired by the Pophams between 1776, when it was still glebe land, and 1806. See above, T330. The name Woollard Hill provides yet another possibility of a name applied at one time to the wider locality.

T333 Winyards. (87 A2) Still glebe land in 1839, when it was shown as an arable strip of one acre. As it was about 290 yards long, it could only have been about 16 yards wide. The 1806 map gives the impression it was just a trackway leading up from the one shown on the 1776 map at the bottom of the hill.

T334 Hix's Mead. (87 A2) Glebe land in 1776, and just marked 'Freehold' in 1806: another sale, probably by a Daubeny.

T335 Woollard Hill. (87 A2) Listed as At the Hick Mead in the 1776 survey. The map shows three divisions within the field in 1776. Like most of the strips on this hill, from 339 round to 316, this division represents a point roughly half way down, making strips of lengths of about 160 to 200 yards.

T336 Field. (87 A2) Owned by 'Bolter' in 1776, not Popham, so not listed in the 1776 survey or shown on the 1806 map.

T337 Oat Hills. (87 A2) Probably the two fields referred to as Hick Mead on page 22 of the 1776 survey, marked on the map as Stratton, after the tenant then. The 1806 map shows this as Hicks Meadow, with furrows following the contours, NW to SE.

T338 Field. (87 A2) Hick Meads in 1776, but apparently not Popham-owned then or in 1806. In 1839 owned by John Gales (see T310, and the introductory section on 'Ownership') the second largest landowner in the parish at that time.

T339 New Close. (87 A2) Hick Meads in 1776, and also in 1806. The 1776 survey says 'At the Hick Mead'. See T326.

T340 New Close. (87 A1) Also New Close in 1776 and 1806. The name would suggest perhaps an 18th century enclosure, but the irregular line of the hedge suggests an earlier date, 16th or 17th century. This was probably rough grazing marking the edge of the arable area, and T340, 341, 389, 390 and 394 probably formed one block of unhedged pasture at the time New Close was enclosed, funnelling to the track by T309.

T341 Ring Pits. (87 A1) Shown as Ring Pit in 1776 and 1806. Probably derived from the circular mark left by an old bell pit or pits (see T168), rather than from a ring of pits. The lane adjoining this field is now called Ringspit lane, referred to above (T301) as the land leading to Casebrook.

T342 Ring Pits. (87 A1) Shown as Glebe land in 1839, but shown as 'Dickinson's Land' in 1806, and no ownership indicated on the 1776 map

T343 Black Rock. (87 A1) Shown within the area generally referred to as 'The Black Rocks' in 1776, owned by Mr Russell in 1776 and by Dickinson in 1806, and by John Gales in 1839. Along the hedgebank of this part of Blackrock Lane there was still be a small amount of Spiked Star-of-Bethlehem (Ornithogalum Pyrenaicum) in the 1980s, in the place where it was recorded in 1912 by J.W.White as its most westerly site in Europe.

T344 As above. (87 A1)

T345 As above. (87 A2)

T346 Long Croft. (87 A1) Long Croft in 1776, and Long Ground in 1806, and Long Ground in 1806.

T347 Black Rock. (86 B2) Shown as 'Charlton' on the 1776, not Popham land and so not on the survey. Also not on the 1806 survey, and just shown as 'freehold' on the map. In 1839 this was the most south westerly of John Gale's holdings, which formed the greater part of the northern tip of the parish. The Wansdyke forms the southern boundary of T347, see the introductory section on The Wansdyke.

T348 Meadow. (86 B2) The Mead in 1776 and The meadow in 1806. The Wansdyke runs along the side of this field, and was the scene of excavations here in 1995 - see the introductory section on the Wansdyke, and the photographs on pages 16 and 17.

T349 Upper Ground. (86 B2) As in 1776 and 1806.

T350 Tining. (86 B2) Tineing in 1776, and Tyning in 1806. Between 1806 and 1839, strips shown on the 1776 map on the south and west of the field were incorporated into it. The Wansdyke runs along the south of the field. At the north western corner of the field is the crossing of Ringspit Lane with Casebrook, two strong and ancient features. Their junction might have been taken as the principal landmark in defining the north western boundary of Publow. Ringspit Lane at this point was almost certainly one of those referred to by Ann Tyler when recalling her childhood at Amercombe House: 'Near us were several deep old lanes, where gipsies used to encamp and stay a week or more, making chairs, baskets, and clothes pegs, the women going round the villages with baskets, selling various small articles and brushes'. [100] The description was written in 1916, and probably refers to the mid-19th century. Ref 'Tyning', see T106.

T351 Black Rock. (86 B2) Shown as 'Dickinson' on the 1776 map, and as 'Taints Land' on the 1806 map.

T352 Black Rock. (86 B2) As in 1776 and 1806.

T353 Black Rock. (86 B2) Not on 1776 survey, probably owned by Dickinson or Mr Russell.

T354 Triangle Piece. (86 B2) As above.

T355 Black Rock. (86 B2) 'Lord Paulett's land' in 1776, but probably not very accurately drawn on the 1776 map. By 1806 it was shown as Taint's land.

T356 Upper Black Rock. (86 B1) Not on the 1776 survey, but shown as Black Rock on the 1806 map, as arable with furrows surprisingly going crossways.

T357 Gunter Mead. (86 B1) Shown as Taints Land in 1806, and not shown on the 1776 survey. Similar names occur at T359 (Gunter Mead), and 360 (Gunder Mead). T359 was referred to as Gundle Mead c1770, and one of the fields the other side of the parish boundary in Stanton Drew is also called Gunter Mead. It seems possible that there is the remnant of a field system here which pre-dates the parish boundary as it existed in 1776 etc. Gunter would seem a probable surname derivation, but the earlier form and the application to a wider area suggest that perhaps the original form might have meant something. The pattern of fields here resembles medieval open field, but there is no obvious settlement or focus to which it might have related. The pattern appears to post-date Ringspit Lane.

T358 Hedge Grove. (86 B1) This field is nowhere near the land of the 1776 tenant named Hedges, and may be derived from hedges, then a grove, that grew up on neglected arable strips. By 1806 the field was arable, and it seems to have been arable for most or all of the years up to 1839. This is one of the many fields in Publow for which detailed crop records for the years 1828-44 have survived. The record of Hedge Grove is representative of that of many arable fields in that period. The crops grown each year from 1828 to 1844, in chronological order, were: wheat, beans, teazels, teazels, wheat, turnips, wheat, teazels, beans, fallow, fallow, beans, oats, beans, turnips, potatoes, wheat. [101] On the 1806 map the field was called Black Rock, and it was not on the 1776 survey.

T359 Gunter Mead. (86 B1) See above, T357. This field retained its reverse 's' outline until at least 1911. That shape is often associated with that of medieval furlongs, following the path taken in preparation for turning at the end of the furrow. The length of this one, about 380 yards, might be unusual.

T360 Gunder Mead. (86 B1) See above, T357. In the field immediately to the west of this, by the A37, a test borehole was drilled in 1951. Pensford No 1 seam was struck at 1,724 foot, No 2 at 1,884 foot, and No 3 at 1,889 foot below sea level (add 221 foot for depth below surface). [A12] Naturally, all the old local bell pits had been tapping into much shallower seams of coal.

T361 Usley Hill. (86 B1) Also shown as Usley Hill on the 1776 map, although the shape of the field was different then. The 1776 map does not show the line of the turnpike road to Bristol, but the 1806 map does. In 1806 it followed the line of the little road between T363 and 364, and carried straight over Gibbett Lane, joining the line of the present A37 just north west of T369. The line of the road between T366 and 367 and between 364 and 361 may have been built in the 1820s. Another slice was taken off the hill with the construction of the present route, in the 1950s. The name Usley was applied in 1839 to T361, 362, 364, and 383. T371 was called 'Tining by Usley Hill'. The name Hursley (Hill) was applied to 366, 367, 369, 376 and 381.

The 1776 and 1806 maps only refer to the area subsequently shown as T361 and 362 as Usley, and neither use the name Hursley. The earliest form so far noted is the Ursley from 1671 (see page 2). The -ley element implies the possibility of Saxon woodland clearance (see page 1). The first element could perhaps be derived from the OE 'Hyrst', a wood particularly on a slope. Vince Russett notes: 'loss of the medial 'r' is not uncommon in modern English, western dialect -for example 'wuss' for worse, 'hoss' for horse'. [55] Alternatively, the various forms could all be derived from an OE person name. With regard to the original site of the suspected Saxon clearance, it might have been the side of the hill and the area below, rather than the area on top of the hill. Ursley Hill would then be the hill above Ursley, just as Publow Hill and Woollard Hill are the hill above Publow and Woollard, etc. By 1885 a small plantation had been planted along the northern edge of T361 and 362, probably on the steep edge of the new turnpike road.

T362 Usley Hill, as above. (86 B1)

T363 Plantation. (86 B1) This is not shown on the 1776 map, but on the 1806 map there is a little note saying: 'A small piece here belonging to this Estate having been formerly cut off by the Road'. This implies a still earlier line of the road, to the west of this piece, and the probable line of this can be made out from aerial photographs, going straight up from the A37 to the north west corner of T364.[72]

T 364 Usley Hill, as above. In 1911 this was sold as 'a piece of valuable accommodation pasture land and old quarry', the plot also including T363 and the line of the old turnpike road. The 'old quarry' is not shown on the 1885 map, or the geological map, although extensive old limestone workings are shown on the latter immediately north west of here. The regular disturbance of the limestone in the vicinity has made this one of the most interesting places for wild flowers in the parish - and J.W.White listed several unusual species as occurring at 'Ursleigh Hill', when he published 'The Bristol Flora' in 1912. Avon Wildlife Trust intermittently cuts back some of the ash encroaching on the site. Despite this, some of the flora species are declining here partly because some of them benefit by soil disturbance, which has not happened much since the new road was made, and perhaps because of thoughtless people picking the flowers.

T365. (86 B1) Not listed on the Tithe Apportionment, presumably regarded as waste, and just off the map in 1806 and 1776. The 1806 map does show that before the turnpike road was rerouted (see T361), Blackrock Lane, coming up from Publow, curved round along the line of the south west boundary of T365. With the new turnpike, Blackrock Lane was diverted slightly to the west, while the part to the north of the new road was diverted slightly to the north, thereby becoming Gibbet Lane. The lane from the east was also diverted slightly to the north, from its original line, along the edge of T379. In other words, on the 1806 map, this lane joined Blackrock Lane round about the tip of T383. The tithe map shows how these changes created T365 as the leftover corner of one formerly rectangular field, the other leftovers being T366 and 367. Similarly the tiny strip on the edge of T365 is marked 377, and was part of another, adjacent rectangular field. By 1866, both T365 and the strip on the edge of it were counted as one piece, and sold to Francis Leyborne Popham, along with the line of the old turnpike road, by the Bristol Turnpike Trustees. The deeds state that this area had been used lately as a 'Turnpike Stone Depot'.[53] In 1866 or 1867 Popham paid £10 for both bits of land, then in 1911 T365 was sold as a building plot for £40.

T366 See above. (86 B1)

T367 See above. (86 B1)

T368 Stockers Two Acres. Not on the 1776 map, but referred to as Stock Tyning on the 1806 map. A Mr Stocker was one of the major tenant farmers in 1776, with the homestead at T282 (Publow Farm). An Anthony Stocker was one of the local Justices of the Peace at the Quarter Sessions held at Wells in January 1630.

T369 Hursley Hill.(87 A1) Not on the 1806 map, and within the area generally referred to as Charlton Field on the 1776 map.

T370 Nine Ground Lane. (87 A1) Nine Ground could possibly be an alternative name for this particular block of Charlton Field. Looking for nine grounds (fields), there are various ways this almost square block of fields could have been divided into nine. The road running across this block seems, from the 1839 map, to post-date the field pattern, but the 1806 map is more convincing in suggesting the reverse. North of T370, off the tithe map and the 1776 map, but included in the 1806 map, is Little Babyland, and a little further east Babyland. This latter name crops up on the 1776 survey, despite not being on the map. It occurs in several other parishes, and English Field Names offers two possible derivations: 1) 'Babba's arable land' (Babba is an OE person name, and Baber still being a frequent local surname. The '-land' element in place names is often associated with 'new arable land' created from the 7th to 12th centuries) or 2) Babylon - a remote part of the parish (there is a Babylon in Winford parish at ST541606).

T371 Tining by Usley Hill. (87 A1) Tyning on the 1806 map, which shows the middle strip (T372) as glebe land; this glebe must have been sold or exchanged by 1839.

T372 Land. See above. (87 A1)

T373 Harry's Tining. (87 A1) Not on 1776 or 1806 maps.

T374 Field. (87 A1)

T375 By Five Acre Tining. (87 A1) Probably a reference to T381, which is 5.3.2 arp, although it is only referred to as Field in 1839. Not on the 1776 map. See T370. 376 Hursley Hill. See T361. Shown as glebe land in 1839, but not shown as glebe land in 1806. Perhaps acquired as an exchange for 372?

T377 West of Parsons. (86 B1) Shown as two plots on the 1806 map.

T379 Plot. See above, T370. (90 B1)

T380 By Charlton Field. (86 B1)

T381 Field. (87 A1) Probably referred to as Five Acre Tining, see T375.

T382 Hursley Hill. (86 B1) See T361.

T383 Usley Hill. (86 B1) See T361 and 365.

T384 Crossway. (87 A1) Just shown as Dickinson land on the 1776 map, and omitted from the 1806 map. Derivation, evidently, from the crossing of Blackrock Lane and Ringspit Lane.

T385 Limekiln Ground. (87 A1) Limekiln Close in 1806 and just Limekiln in 1776. Limekilns were often associated with 18th century enclosure, and the word 'close', combined with the regular shape of the field suggests an enclosure of that date. The rest of the area between here and T369 might have been laid out earlier than this. At any rate, the whole block, with the exception of T370, was arable in 1839. See also T164 and 165 and 393. 386 Field. Omitted from the 1776 and 1806 maps.

T387 Lypeat. (87 A1) Glebe land, so not directly referred to in 1776, though the survey mentions 'A Close in Charlton by Lippit Gate'. The map roughly indicates Lippit Gate as being on the crossroads here. The 1806 map shows Lypiate Gate as the triangle of land north east of T391, just off the map. Successive OS maps have moved Lypiatt further and further down the road. In 'The Natural History of Chew Valley' (1987) Michael Costen wrote: 'Minor names connected with conserved woodland, such as 'lipyeat' (hlip gate), a 'leap gate' devised to allow animals out of the woodland but not into it are reasonably common in the field names in the district'. A further article in the book suggests that this Lypiatt could have marked the southern edge of Filton, or Fillwood Chase. [102] This chase could have extended from Hengrove to Keynsham in medieval times, although the word may have denoted a non-royal 'forest' rather than necessarily extensive woodland. The precise extent or former extent of this chase is unlikely to ever be known - even John Norden failed to establish this in a survey of 1615:

'For wante of the boundarie and perambulation of the same chace I could by noe examination find the extente. But it is proved by other that the deere raunging out of the forest over the river of Avon freely and without disturbance feed as farr as Dundry hilles neer 4 myles from the forest of Kingswood and in divers places between the said hills and the forest. But time and discontinuaunce of use have forgotten the names, altered the bounds and lost the lands formerly knowne and used and injoyed as belonginge unto his Majesty's Chace of Fillwoode'. [103]

This particular field, T387, was one of those plots of glebe land bought by Popham from Daubeny in 1846 (see T7). The convergence of five, maybe seven, tracks here implies the possibility of a significant ancient feature.

T388 Hilly Corner. (87 A1)

T389 Black Rock. (87 A1) Not on the 1806 map, and just shown as 'Mr Whippey' on the 1776 map. Mr Whippey was not a tenant of the Pophams and does not appear in the 1776 survey, and neither does the Mr Russell shown as owning land near here. With regard to the speculation above (T347), it would be interesting to know if Messrs Whippey and Russell lived in, or had more lands in, Queen Charlton. A Thomas Whippey was noted as the bailiff of FyIton (ie Whitchurch) in the Valor Ecclesiasticus entry for Keynsham Abbey, in 1535. [104] Only one entry of this name has been noted on the Publow parish registers, with a daughter of Sarah Whippie and John Whatley baptised in 1769.

T390 Sheep Hill. (87 A1) Clearly shown and listed as Steep Hill in 1776 and Slip Hill in 1806! See above, T340.

T391 Black Rock. (87 A1) Just shown as Lord Paulett's land in 1776 and 1806.

T392 Charlton Field. (87 A1) The rectangular projection on the north east length of this field relates to furlongs roughly indicated on the 1776 map with the note 'Charlton Field'. This is further evidence that the apparently clear boundary shown on the 1839 map may not always have been so clear. The 1806 map shows how the furlongs exists either side of the road here.

T393 Lime Kiln Paddock. (87 B1) Glebe land, another one of the plots bought by Popham in 1846, see T7. The adjacent field is also called after a lime kiln: presumably both burnt blue or white lias from the plateau, in order to spread the lime on the fields below and to the west.

T394 Lime Kiln Ground. (87 B2) The same name in 1806, and just Lime Kiln in 1776. See above, and T340.

T395 Stockers. (87 B2) Named after the Publow Farm Mr Stocker, probably (see T368), although the strip belonged to Dickinson in 1776.

T396 Field. (87 B2) Dickinson's land in 1776.

T397 Piece. (87 A2) Listed as 'Called Three Lands' in 1776.

T398 Field. (87 A2) Marked Stocker on the map, but shown as 'At the Hick Mead' on the 1776 survey, and annotated 1.2.38 arp 'claimed by Bolter'.

T399 Starve Acre. (87 B2) Also shown as Starve Acre on the 1776 and 1806 maps. The name is a fairly common one, normally implying poor crops.

T400 Field. (87 B2) Part Dickinson's land and part Bolter's land in 1776.

T401 Field. (87 B2) Part Dickinson's Land and part waste - a roadside waste of two acres as indicated on the 1776 map appropriated or enclosed by 1839. The 1806 map if fact shows a much wider verge on both sides of Woollard Hill and totals the 'waste' at 4.1.28 arp.

T402 Woollard Hill. (87 B2) Shown as Woollard Tineing in 1776. See T106.

T403 Wall Tyning. (87 B2) Not on the 1776 map.

T404 Part of a Field. (87 B2)

T405 Field. (87 B2)

T406 Hill Close. (87 B2)

T407 Field. (87 B2)

T408 Inclosure. (87 B2) Possibly of part of the roadside waste referred to above, T401.

T409 New Inclosure. (87 B2) As above.

T410 Field. (87 B2) Shown on the 1776 map as Capell (see T316). The 1776 map does not clearly indicate the presumed waste on the western edge of T410, but then it is generally vague where non-Popham land is concerned. The arrangement of 'chapel' buildings or holdings on either side of the road would be reminiscent of the two church buildings either side of the road at Woollard, T231 and 232.

T411 Mead Hill. (87 B2) Shown as The Hill on the 1776 map.

REFERENCES etc

The most important collection of documents for the history of Publow is the Popham collection at Somerset Record Office (DD PO, and DD PO t). Another major archive is unfortunately 6,000 miles away - this is the Hastings collection at the Huntington Library in San Marino in California. There is probably a good deal of important material relating to 15th and 16th century Publow and Pensford here. The SRO only has a small number of these documents on microfiche.

In March 2003 the Chief Curator of Manuscripts at The Huntington Library, Mary L. Robertson, replied to my enquiry by noting that there is no full index of documents that might mention Pensford or Publow (the collection is some 50,000 pieces strong so that full subject indexing for correspondence, accounts, or manorial papers is beyond the Library). From the various partial catalogues and handlists, she located only ten deeds, ranging in date from 1413 to 1565. Four of them are already published in volume 1 (pp. 286, 289, 310, 314) of the Historical Manuscript Commission's four volume Report on the Manuscripts of the Late Reginald Rawdon Hastings and in another four, Publow and Pensford appear only as two of numerous manors in many counties. These references are to Pensford and Publow's place in the rich Hungerford inheritance, which came into the Hastings family by marriage in the late 15th century and was administered more or less as a single unit for some time thereafter.

Of the other two deeds, one (Huntington Library reference HAD 2802) records a mortgage of just Pensford and Publow by George, the 1st Earl of Huntington, to the London mercer William Browne for £800 in 1536; the other (HAD 2803) is the sale to Henry Beacher on 2 June 1565. Neither of them says much about the villages themselves, being largely occupied with the financial and legal agreements. There are no court rolls, rentals, religious records, etc. The Library can provide estimates for charges of microfilm copies.

More general secondary sources used extensively for this book include 'English Field Names' (1972) by John Field, from which most of the basic field name dervations have been taken. More recent sources for place name interpretation are the books of Margaret Gelling, listed below. Other earlier sources for place name research are given in Avon Past No.3, 'Place Names in Avon and the South West: A Guide to Current Sources' by Jennifer Scherr. The Journal of the English Place-Name Society should be available for reference at Bristol Library, in case of future work on Somerset (as noted, Somerset is the only English county for which the society has no published study).

References to the Becket Centre, are to an arts centre in Pensford's church, which was made redundant after the floods of 1968 . The Becket Centre and its management Trust failed to raise enough funding to cope with the building's huge repair and maintenance bills, and so the Trust and Arts Centre were wound up in the early 1990s. The historic documents acquired by the Becket Centre were subsequently passed to Pensford History Society.

In the following references, secondary sources are given where they are more accessible than primary sources, and where these give a full reference to the primary source.

The abbreviations used below:
BCCCRL Bristol City Council Central Reference Library
SAM   Sites and Monuments Record, formerly Avon. now B&NES
BRO   Bristol Record Office
SANHS   Somerset Archaeological & Natural History Society, Proceedings
SRO   Somerset Record Office
SRS   Somerset Record Society

Where the dates 1776, 1806, 1839, 1871, 1885,and 1911 are used in the main text without footnotes, the sources are the respective maps and surveys listed below, AI to A13.

AI   SRO: DD/PO 71 (survey of the manors of Pensford, Publow and Woollard, 1776)
A2   SPO: DD/PO 72 (map of the manors of Pensford, Publow and Woollard, 1776)
A3   SRO: DD/PO 73 (map [1806] and survey [1806-7] of the manors of Houndstreet, Marksbury, Chelwood, Farmborough, Compton Dando, Publow and Woollard. Note, this map is in need of repair and will not be available for study until fixed).
A4   SRO: DD/PO 74 (two maps of part of Pensford, one probably 1806, the other probably a fair copy of part of DD/PO 72)
A5   Ordnance Survey, First Edition One Inch to the mile map of Bath and Wells (1817), from a revised copy printed in 1893 and reprinted by David and Charles in 1970.
A6   SRO: DD Rt 112 (tithe map and apportionment of Publow, 1839)
A7   SRO: DD/MER 34 (map of Houndstreet Estate, with survey, 1871)
A8   Ordnance Survey maps, 1:2,500, published in 1885. (Copies at BCCCRL).
A9   Map of Hunstrete Estate, with rent roll, c1906. Various extant copies locally.
A10 Maps of part of Hunstrete Estate with catalogue of sale in 1911. Catalogue reprinted by the Becket Centre in 1986.
A11 SRO: DD/QK 142 c/2984 (maps of part of Hunstrete Estate in sale catalogue of 1917. Another copy at SRO is annotated with prices - DD/SCL 12 c/2426).
A12 Geological survey of ST66NW by G.A.Kellaway 1945-49, published 1960 (scale 1:10,560)
A13 Geological survey of ST66SW, by G.A.Kellaway 1944-9 and F.B.A.Welch 1943-4, published 1973 (scale 1:10,560)

Numercial footnote references:

1   SRS Vol 51 p112
2   Somerset & Dorset Notes & Queries p 213
3   Claire Cross 'The Puritan Earl - The Life of Henry Hastings, Third Earl of Huntingdon, 1536-1595' (1966)
4   SRS Vol 24 p 272
5   G.A.J.Loxton 'Queen Charlton Perambulation - A History' (1999)
6   SRO: DD POt 151
7   Huntington Library: H.A., 6722, 10348
8   Bristol and Avon Archaeological Research Group, 'Parish Surveys of Flax Bourton, Bathford and Queen Charlton'
9   British Museum Add. MSS. 28273.
10 Maurice Cranston 'John Locke, a Biography' (1957)
11 Journal of the British Archaeological Association, Vol 31 (1875) p 204
12 Michael Costen 'The Origins of Somerset' (1992)
13 Margaret Gelling 'Place-Names in the Landscape' (1984).
14 Margaret Gelling and Ann Cole 'The Landscape of Place-Names' (2000).
15 Margaret Gelling, in The Local Historian Vol 23 No 3 (1992) page 124.
16 Rowland Janes (Ed.) 'The Natural History of the Chew Valley' (1987)
17 Oliver Rackham, 'The History of The Countryside' (1986)
18 PRO: MAF 68/59, and MAF 68/60
19 J.W.White, 'The Bristol Flora' (1912)
20 Keith Gardner 'The Wansdyke Diktat? - A Discussion Paper', in Bristol and Avon Archaeology (1998)
21 Jean Manco 'Dobunni to Hwicce', on her website at www.building- history.pwp.blueyonder.co.uk/
22 B.Cunliffe 'Iron Age Communities in Britain: an account of England, Scotland and Wales from the seventh century BC to the Roman conquest 3rd edn' (1991)
23 N.J.Higham 'An English Empire: Bede and the Early Anglo-Saxon Kings' (1995)

24 Charles Brown, pp 18-19 in 'North Wansdyke Past and Present' (Journal of Keynsham and Saltford Local History Society, No.1, 1987)
25 Michael Costen, 'Stantonbury and District in the Tenth Century', pp 25-34 in Bristol and Avon Archaeology 11 (1983)
26 Michael Costen 'Place Name Evidence in South Avon', pp13-17 in Avon Past No. 1 (1979)
27 Brooks N. 'The Formation of the Mercian Kingdom' (1989)
28 SRO: DD PO 22
29 Rob Iles, p 117 in 'The Archaeology of Avon', Ed. Michael Aston and Rob Iles (1987).
30 L.Toulmin Smith, Ed., 'John Leland's Itinerary in England' Vol. 5 (1910).
31 Beatrice Marion Willmott Dobbie 'An English Rural Community' [Bathhampton] (1969)
32 Victoria County History of Somerset, pp 129-131
33 SRS Vol III pp 28 and 91
34 Charles Pooley 'The Old Stone Crosses of Somerset' (1877)
35 SANHS Vol 99 (1954) pp 49-74
36 SRS Vol 23 p 78
37 SRS Vol 28 p 195
38 Edwin Jervoise 'The Ancient Bridges of the South of England' (1930)
39 Michael Aston, p 97 in 'The Archaeology of Avon' (1987)
40 SRS Vol 76
41 Journal of the British Archaeological Association, Vol 31 (1875) p 204
42 SRS Vol 65 p 18
43 SRS Vol 28 p 195
44 SRS Vol 28 p 210
45 SRS Vol 34 p 3
46 SRO: Q/SR 299 (1) 2 (6)
47 An Act for Repairing, widening and improving the several Roads round the City of Bristol, and for making certain new lines of Road to communicate with same', 14th June 1819. (copy in BCCCRL)
48 'Bristol Turnpikes: General Statements for the year ending 25th March 1831' (copy in BCCCRL)
49 SRO: DD/PO 36d
50 John A.Bulley, 'To Mendip for Coal - A Study of the Mendip Coalfield before 1830', in SANHS Vol 97 (1952) p48.
51 Second part of the above paper in SANHS Vol 98 (1953) p 22.
52 Painting by William Curtis, c1840, original in Bristol City Museum (not displayed).
53 SRO: DD/PO 4r
54 BRO: 21789 (21)
55 Vince Russett, pers. com.
56 SRO: DD PO/22
57 SRO: DD/SOG 787
58 SRO: DD/PO 108
59 SANHS Vol 111 (1965)
60 Nicholas Culpepper, 'Complete Herbal' (1653)
61 Somerset Dendrochronology Project (Somerset Vernacular Building Research Group), by Oxford Dendrochronology, see www.dendrochronology.com/
62 Joan Day, 'Bristol Brass' (1973)
63 SRO: DD/PO 36a
64 SRO: DD/OB 106
65 SRS Vol 28 p 302

66 Painting by E.Parkman, c1890, Bath City Gallery (not displayed)
67 SRO: DD/PO t 133
68 Holly (Horace) Batten, notes made in 1987
69 British Museum Add. MSS. 28273
70 SRS Vol 23 p 131 etc
71 Publow Parish Council minutes, 1919 and 1951
72 Aerial photo of 26.9.58 - F21 58 RAF 2597 No 0073
73 Aerial photos, 1946/3g-TUD-UK-1525 5019 and 5020. Also SAM.
74 Vivian Ritson, 'A History of Pensford and Publow' (1913, unpublished)
75 SANHS Vol 77 (1932)
76 SRS Vol 51 p 50
77 SRO: DD/RM Vol 1 (1736-1792)
78 SRO: QS/1/125 2 (1)
79 BRO: 21789 (16)
80 John Billingsley, 'Agricultural Survey of Somerset' (1791)
81 SRO: DD/PO t 31
82 SRS Vol 24 p272
83 Aerial photograph, RP 106G UK 1661 12 July 1946 No 3447
84 Jim Hancock, aerial photograph 5th June 1972
85 SRS Vol 54 p 12
86 SRO: DD/PO 41
87 SRO: DD/Bbm 203 and 335
88 Survey by Commander E.H.D.Williams (1987) copy in SANHS Library
89 Painting by W.W.Wheatley (1864), in Bristol University Library Special Collections Department, with H.S.Thompson's account of the River Chew (1932)
90 BRO: 21789 (14) and (20)
91 SRO: DD/X/BKT C/503 (1659 survey) and DD/S/WH Box 42 (1730 survey)
92 SRO: DD/BR/1 ch
93 Margaret Gelling, 'Signposts to the Past' (1988)
94 SRO: DD/PO 4b c/62
95 BRO: 20132/98
96 Bristol and Avon Archaeological Research Group, 'Parish Surveys of Flax Bourton, Bathford and Queen Charlton'
97 Victoria County History of Somerset, Vol II p 405
98 Bath Natural History and Field Club Proceedings Vol I p 35
99 J.Collinson, 'The History and Antiquities of Somerset' (1791)
100 Bristol Times and Mirror 8.4.1916, p 1
101 SRO: DD/PO 107
102 'The Natural History of the Chew Valley' (1987) p 28
103 Quoted in Victoria County History of Somerset
104 'Valor Ecclesiasticus' (1535). Record Commission transcript (1810) Vol. I p 181 (copy in ACCCRL)
105 G.B.Grundy, 'The Saxon Charters and Field Names of Somerset' (1935)
106 SRS Vol 23 pages 183 and 200, SRS Vol 24 pages 12 and 222
107 SRO: DD/PO t 31
108 Elizabeth White, 'Keynsham and Saltford, Life and Work in Times Past, 1539-1945' (1990) page 16. Also pers.comm.
109 Michael Heaton, Historic Building Record, September 2000
110 SRO: DD/SOG 787

INDEX OF FIELD NAMES etc, to Tithe number references

Alderwells 103,104,109
Amercam 294
Amercombe 350
Babyland 370
Bakers 200,201,207
Barham, Long 15
Barhams 16
Barken 207
Beadams 134
Beadons 134
Bell Inn 231
Birchwood 130,131,166,167,176
Bitham 134
Black Rock 343 etc
Blackrock Lane 365
Blues 117
Bookhill 200,201,202,203,204
Borough Bank 316
Broomy, Great 238
Burdons 135
Butts 12,289,290
Butts Markham 11
Butts Meadow 5
Butts Orchard 288
Calves Close 108
Capell 316,317,340
Carsbrook 301,350
Casebrook 301,350
Catley 108
Cave's 108
Chapel Piece 131
Charlton Field 214,370,380,392
Chelwood Gate 152
Church Lands 136,137,161,172
Clarelew 298
Coalpit 174 etc
Common 128,130,197,274,298 etc
Cowman Mead 97,98
Coneygre 45a,125,132,140,210
Copeland 18
Corn Close 107
Corn Leaze 296
Crabtree Close 114
Crossway 384
Cuckow Sleight 329
Daffy's 207,216,217
Drake's Close 207
Ducknest 98
Duckpools, Mr Owen's 98
Gallows Close 153

George Inn 86
Gibbett Lane 361
Gorse 303
Greens Folly 85
Grove 10, 111,127, 129, 131, 215, 218,303
Gunder Mead 357,359
Gundle mead 357,359
Ham 14,15,219 etc
Halfpenny Well 40
Hawkham 308
Hedge Grove 358
Hedge mead 268
Hedges 279,306
Henpound 102,208
Hermitage 282
Herns 172
Hick 329,335,337,338,339 etc
Hickley 305
Hix 326,334
Holkham 308
Hollybushes 116
Ham Meads 118
Hursley 361,366,367,369,376,381
K's 108
Ketchey's 305
Keynsham 102
Kinsham 102
Leigh 122
Lime Close 307,308,311,312
Lime Pits 330
Limekiln 164,165,168,393,394,385
Lords Wood 173
Lye 110,120,122,198,199 etc
Lydown 126,133
Lyfield 115
Lypeat 387
Magnet 241
Marcombe 14
Markham 11, 14
Mill Mead 154,186,191
Mooncroft 140
Moorcroft 115,140
Mountain 219,220
Nine Ground Lane 370
Oat Hills 337
Oatley Close 108
Paradise Row 85,253,254,255
Pensford Down 45a
Petty Close 309
Pipershill 155,159

Pond Close 182,183
Pool Mead 126
Pound 3,4
Pound Close 116
Priest Dam 247,262
Pris Down 247,274
Pryors Hill 163
Publow Common 197
Publow Hill 96,246
Publow Wood 105
Ring Pits 341,342
Ringspit 341,350
Rowler's 278
Rush Mead 290
Salters Brook 40
Sandhills 110, 138, 139, 141
Sandhole 110
Seagrove 215,218
Shutty Mead 124
Sideham 58
Sideland 295
Sidelong 295
Sidon 58
Starve Acre 399
Stout's Mead 194
Stratton Hill 14
Summer Leaze 287
Tanyard 232
Tining/Tyning 106, 350, 371,373, 375, 403
Usley Hill 361,362,364,383
Vineyard 313,314,315
Walls Mead 195
Ware Pool 209
Wethergroves 154
Whitley 150,151
Whitley Batch 162
Winyards 331 etc
Winyards Hill 318 etc
Woollard Hill 332,335

INDEX OF NAMES OF PEOPLE

Adams, A. - T116
Baber - T370
Baber, Francis - T91
Batt, Mary - T151, T168
Batten, Holly - T91
Baum, F. - T63, T143
Bellamy, Rev A. - T97, T210, T265
Bilk, Acker - T281
Billingsley, John - T164
Bisse, John - T5
Blanning, Ann - T84
Blanning, Henry-T84
Bokeland, John - T200
Bokke, Willelmo - T200
Boleyn, Ann - T7-10
Bolter - T336
Bridges, Sir Thomas - T91
Bright, Richard - T209
Broadrip,Mr - T164, T168
Brown, Richard - T130
Bullock, Richard - T161
Cave, James - T108
Clare, Gilbert de - T298
Copeland, - T18
Corp, Susanna - T18
Cottle, Mr - T218, T301
Culpepper, Nicholas - T58
Curtis, William - T1
Daubeny, Reverend Andrew - T7-10
Daubeny, Reverend James - T7-10
Dickinson Vickris - T309, T318-T325, T400, T401
Duckett, Cornelius - T232
Duckett, Miriam - T232
Duckett, William - T232
Fifoot, John - T290
Fifoot, Martha - T290
Flower, William - T33
Freeman Esquire - T209
Gales, John - T309, T325, T338, T343, T347
Green, Martha - T29
Green, Daniel - T85
Green, James - T29
Green, John - T29
Green, Richard - T29
Hanney, George - T162
Harris, Ezekiel - T84
Harwar, Nicholas - T142
Hawting, Mr - T122

Heath, Joseph - T33
Hedges, T268, T279
Herne, William - T172
Hodges, William - T231
Hudson, C. - T43
Jeffreys, Lord Chief Justice - page
John Freeman & Copper Co - T85
Kent, N. - T210
Langford, Mr - T236
Leech, Roger - T17, T32
Lloyd, William - T293, T330
Lock, Edward - T14, T86
Lock, Peter - T14
Locke, John - T14, T86
Long, Lambrook - T91
Norden, John - T391
Owen, Mr - T98, T212, T218
Parkman E. - T90
Parr, Katherine - T7-10
Paulet, Lord - T293, T355
Pearce, Richard - T164
Pine, James - T248
Popham, Alexander - T210
Popham, Dorothy - T58
Popham, Edward - T162, T231, T309
Popham, Francis - T130
Popham, Sir Francis - T166, T174
Popham, Francis Leyborn - T210, T265, T365
Pophams, T29
Price, William - T174
Primrose, Henry - T33
Ralph, Bishop - T313
Ritson, Vivian - T298, T281
Russell, Mr - T343
Sage, Henry - T18 T313
Seymour Lord Thomas - T7-10
Smart, Annie - T33
Smart, Doris - T33
Smart, George - T33
Smith, William - T209
Stocker - T116, T368, T395
Stocker, Anthony - T368
Sweetman - T155
Taint, Sir Charles - T216, T293, T288, T293, T294
Taylor, Mr - T204
Tyler, Ann - T350
Tyndall & Co - T183
Tyndall and Elton - T85
Ward, George - T85
Ward, Mary - T85
Ward, Richard Brickdale - T85

Weeks, James - T232
Wesley, John - T20, T250, T274
Whatley, John - T389
Wheatley,W.W. - T232
Whippey - T389
Whippey, Thomas - T389
Whippie, Sarah - T389
White, J.W. - T58, T102, T173, T343, T364

Some further lists are due to be posted on Biografix website later in 2003 - see www.biografix.co.uk
These may include:

1901 Census: Names and ages for Publow parish

1839 Tithe apportionment: Names of landowners and tenants in Publow parish.

1776 Popham Estate Survey (DD PO 71): Names of landowners and tenants in Publow parish.

Tithe Map of 1839
pages 86 to 91
Note, there are a few slight inaccuracies in these copies, due to various imperfections in the original photocopying, and consequent problems in perfectly matching all the sections of the map.

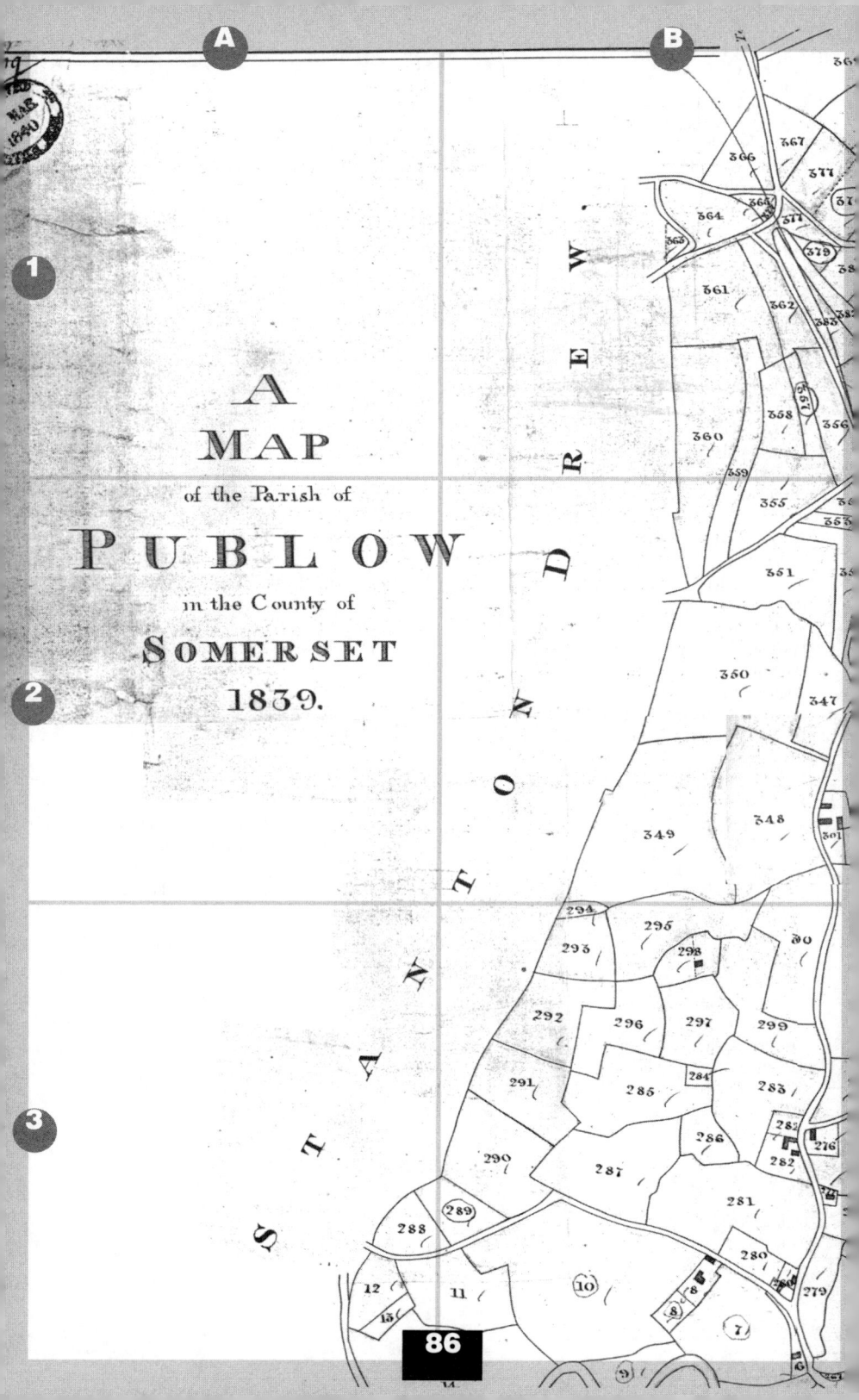

A MAP of the Parish of PUBLOW in the County of SOMERSET 1839.

QUEEN CHARLTON

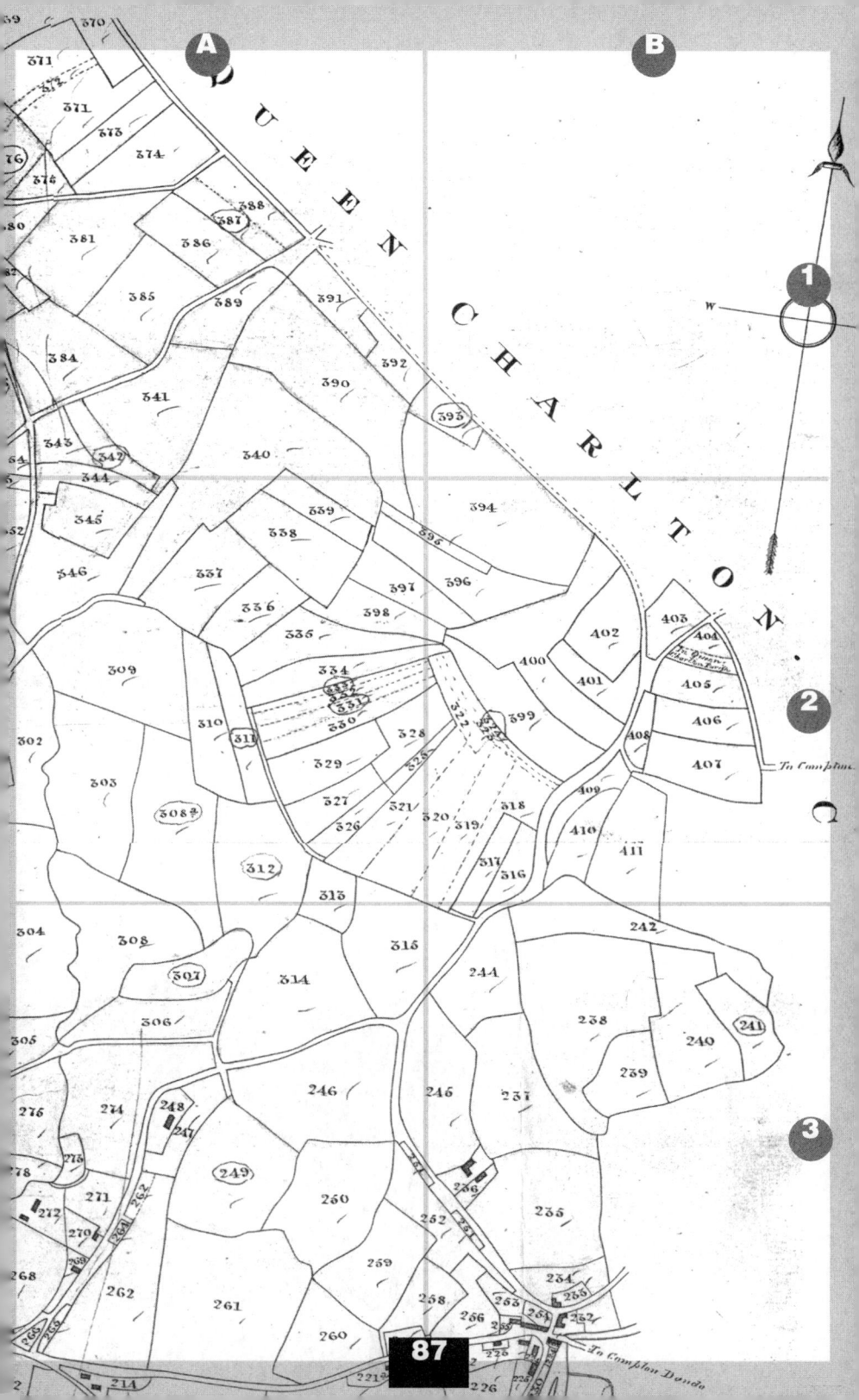

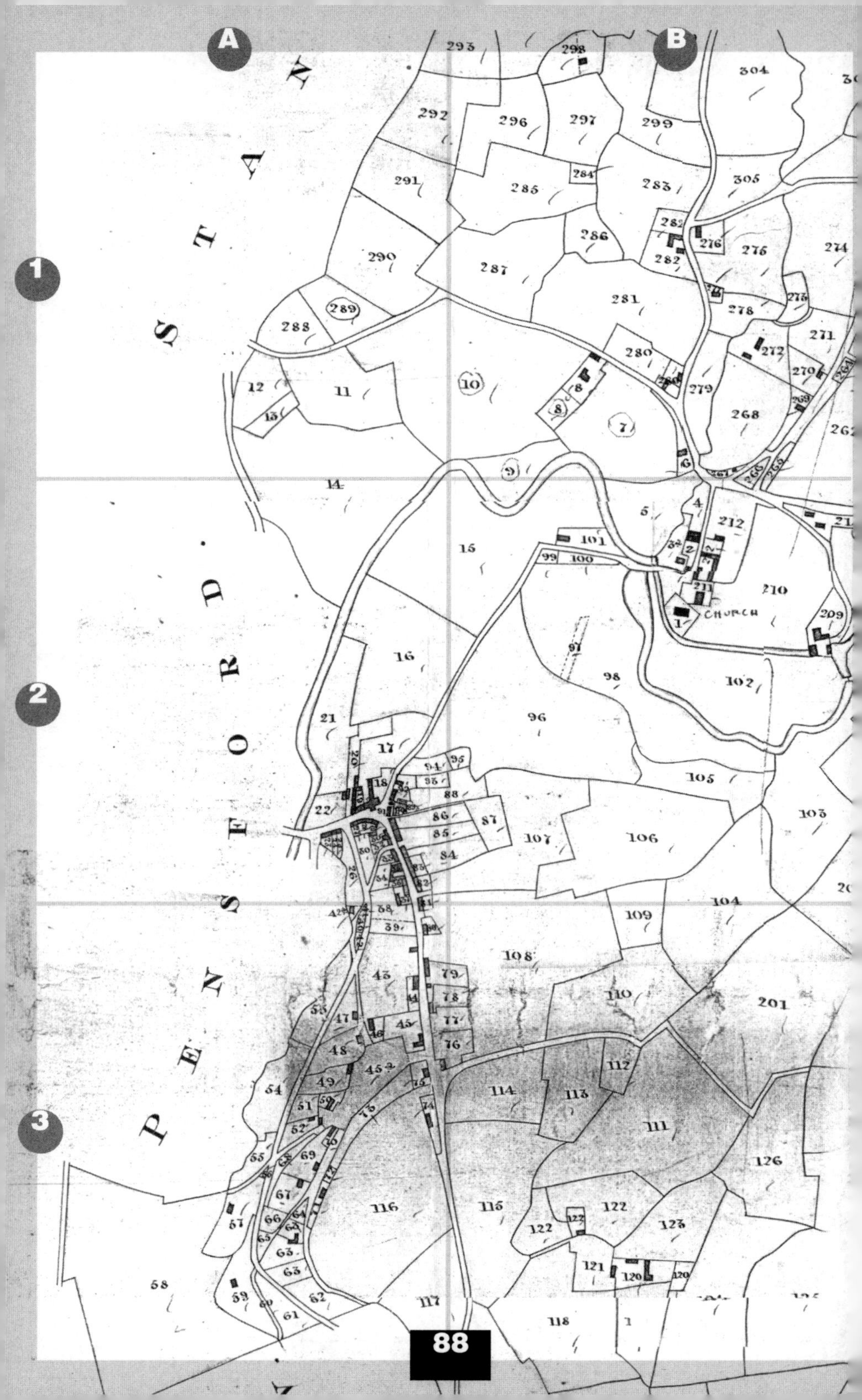
A
B
1
2
3
PENSFORD STAN
CHURCH

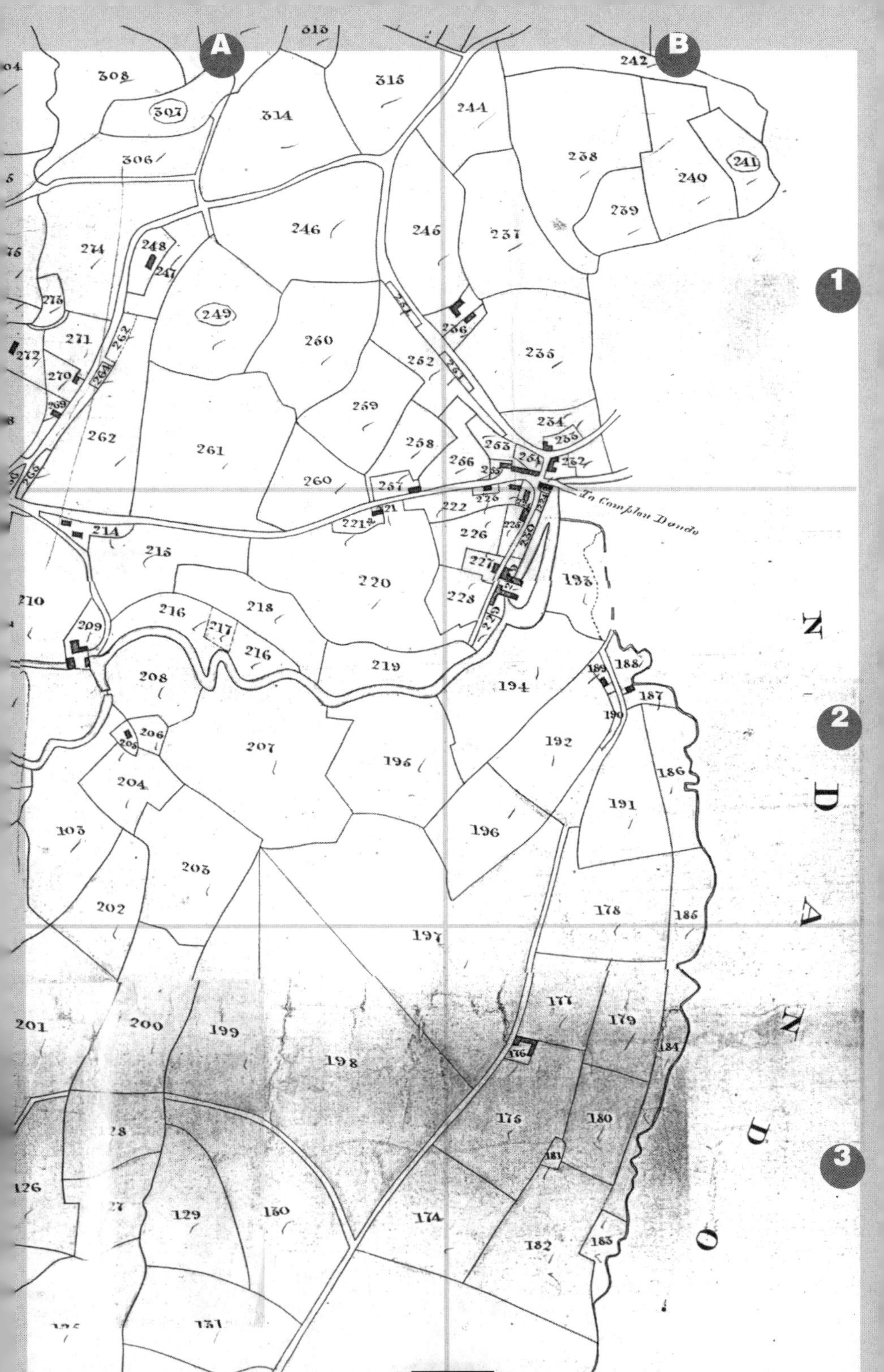
A
B
1
2
3
To Compton Dando
N
D
A
N
D
O

90

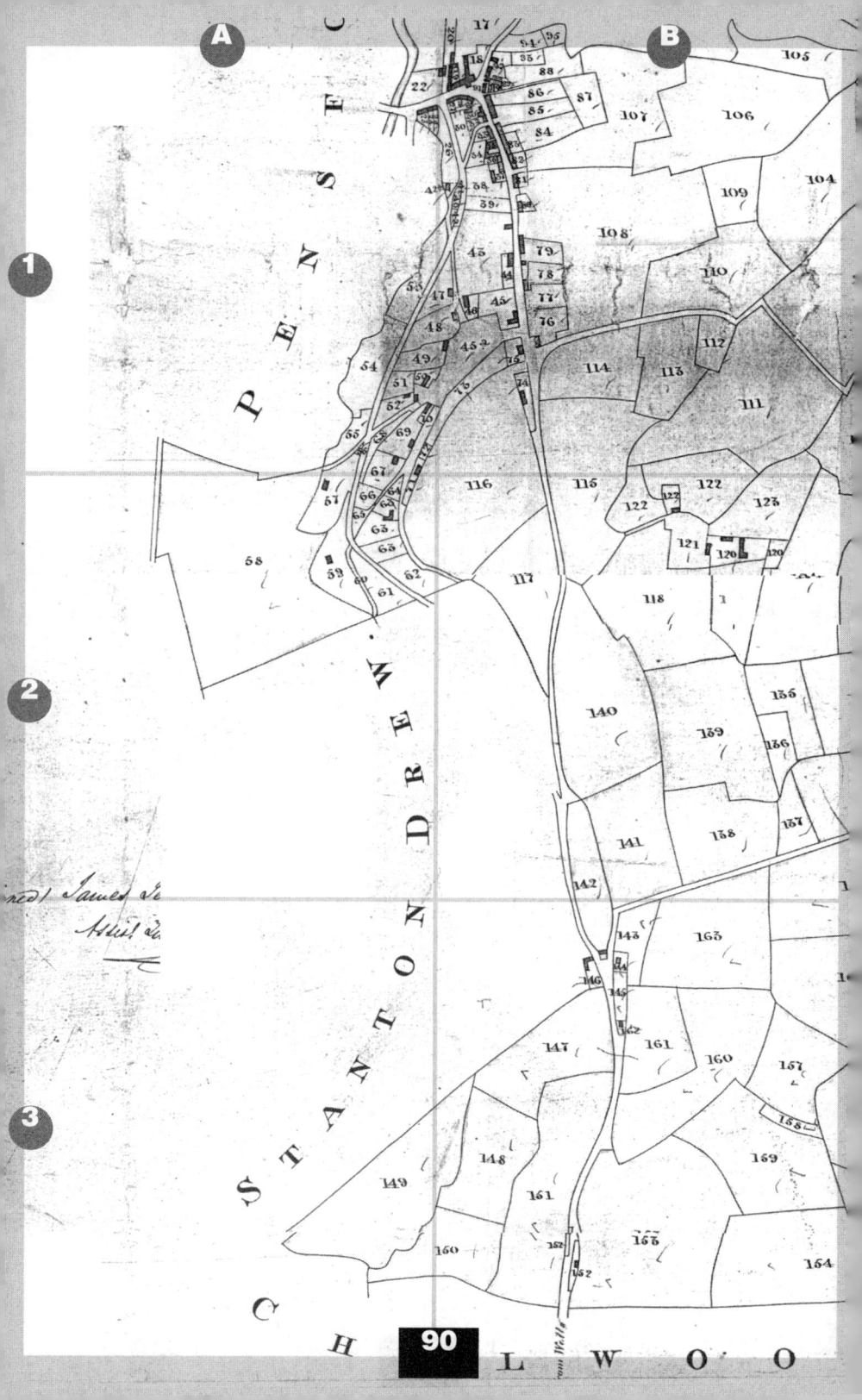

91

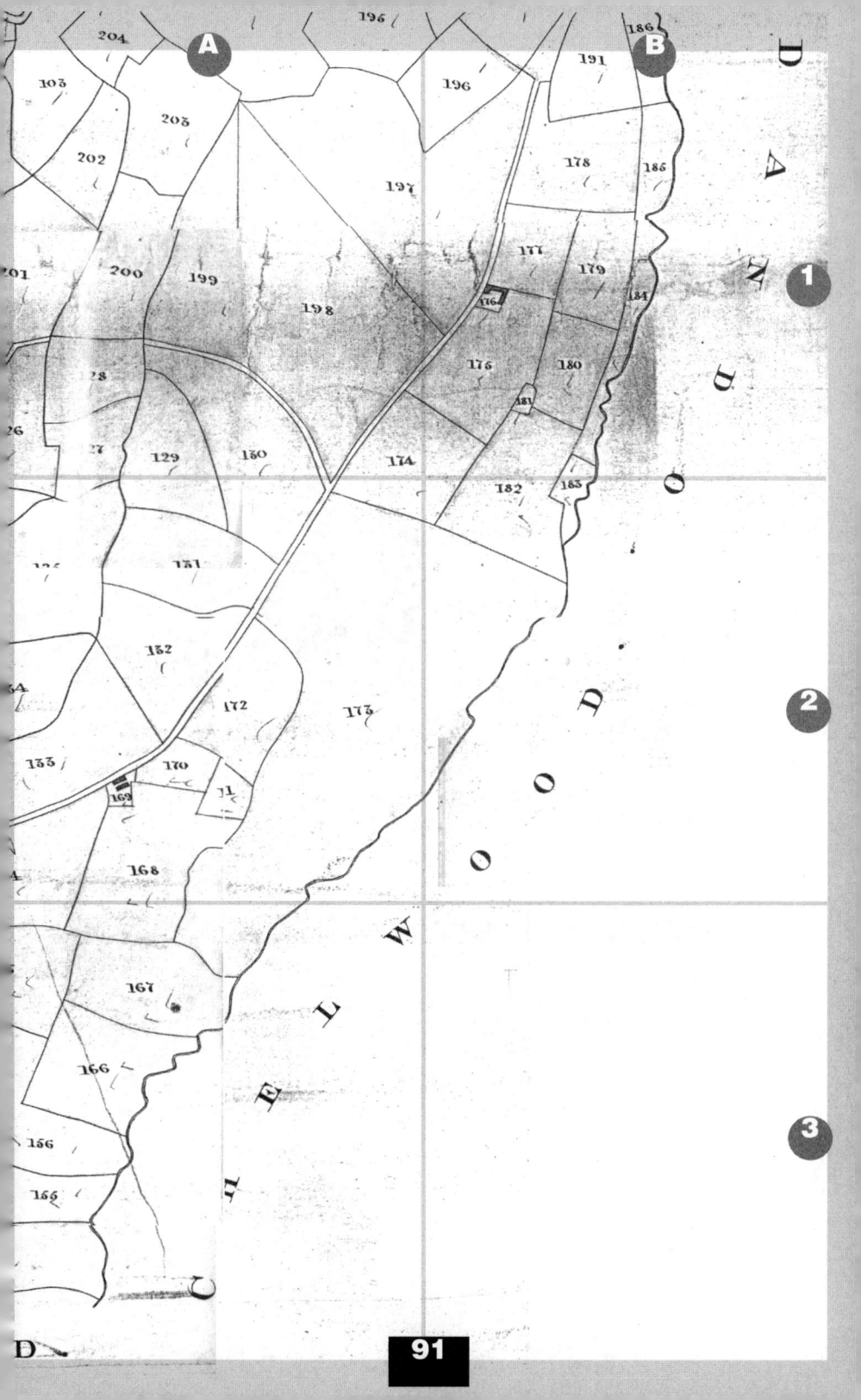

INFO FOR VISITORS

Pensford Pubs
The George and Dragon
01761 490516
The Rising Sun
01761 490402
The Travellers Rest
01761 490347

Tourist Information
The Pensford area is an ideal base for exploring the big three tourist cities of Bath, Bristol and Wells, as it is more or less midway between the three. More info from:
- Bath
01225 477101
www.visitbath.co.uk
- Bristol
0906 7112191 (premium rate)
www.visitbristol.co.uk
- Wells
01749 672552
www.mendip/gov.uk

Village website
www.pensford.com

Ordnance Survey Maps
Explorer 155 (2.5 inches to the mile)
Landranger 172 (1.25 inches to the mile)

A stile and steps on the footpath from the A37 road up to fields near the former site of the old village green, see T45, page 39. The photograph was taken in 1996 soon after the stile was installed (see acknowledgements, page 3). The path is number 19 on the map on page iii.